PENGUIN HANDBOOKS PH54

The Cool Greenhouse

G. W. ROBINSON

Greenhouses have been in continuous use in this country since the seventeenth century and this is evidence enough that they are useful. From the stone built 'orangery', the present type of glass-house, and with it methods of heating, were gradually improved, reaching their peak in the huge timber and iron structures of the last century.

Today we have keener competition than ever, new materials, light airy construction and automatic heating, ventilating, and even watering. These are in fact exciting times for the gardener as every year sees new developments designed to take the drudgery out of horticulture and to make maintenance easier.

In the greenhouse the gardener can cultivate a much wider range of plants than is possible in the open, and this book is written in the hope that it will foster interest in both plants and their culti-vation and perhaps encourage gardeners to venture with new plants.

Mr Robinson clearly describes a wide selection of suitable plants from chrysanthemums to orchids. The rarer choice plant, however, is not forgotten. He also gives suggestions for the kind of glasshouse to choose for particular purposes, how to heat it, and how to propagate and cultivate plants in it.

General Editor: Patrick M. Synge.

The cover illustration shows a group of cool greenhouse plants, photographed by Miss Valerie Finnis.

A fine group of the lovely golden-yellow arum *Zantedeschia pentlandii* which is more tender than the common white arum, but is a beautiful greenhouse plant. See p. 164

G. W. ROBINSON

THE COOL GREENHOUSE

Prepared in conjunction and collaboration with
The Royal Horticultural Society

PENGUIN BOOKS

Penguin Books Ltd, Harmondsworth, Middlesex
U.S.A.: Penguin Books Inc., 3300 Clipper Mill Road, Baltimore 11, Md
AUSTRALIA: Penguin Books Pty Ltd, 762 Whitehorse Road, Mitcham, Victoria

First published 1959

Made and printed in Great Britain by
Jarrold & Sons Ltd, Norwich

Contents

List of Plates

9

List of Text Figures

11

Author's Acknowledgements

Mr J. E. Downward provided the majority of the photographs and his trouble and care are gratefully acknowledged. The author's thanks are also due to the following for providing suitable pictures: Mr A. W. Gray and Elsa M. Megson for photographs on electrical heating; Messrs R. A. Malby and Co. of Woodford Green, Essex, Mr Robert M. Adam, Mr W. Abbing, Mr Donald F. Merrett, the Shell Photographic Unit for photographs of pests and diseases; Messrs Allwood Bros. of Haywards Heath for illustrations of carnations; Mr J. B. Stevenson, Mr E. T. Thistlethwaite and the National Chrysanthemum Society for diagrams of chrysanthemums; the Edinburgh and East of Scotland College of Agriculture for the magnificent picture of Rhododendron 'Fragrantissimum'; and to the following for photographs of greenhouses or equipment: Concrete Greenhouses Ltd of Marlow, Buckinghamshire; the Crittall Manufacturing Co. Ltd, High Holborn, London WC1; Messrs Duncan Tucker (Tottenham) Ltd, of Tottenham, London E15; Messrs V. and N. Hartley Ltd, of Oldham; Oakworth Greenhouses of Wellington, Shropshire; Shepherd's Aerosols Ltd of Jermyn Street, London SW1; and Messrs John Martin (Staffs) Ltd of Hanley; Messrs G. F. Strawson and Son of Horley, Surrey; and the Sylglass Company of Knight's Hill, London SE27.

Introduction

When taking over a house with an established garden the newcomer is sometimes lucky enough to find a greenhouse or conservatory attached. More often, it is a gradual process of using first a few panes of glass or cloches, then garden frames to shelter and protect particular treasures, and finally the greenhouse. It is often possible to erect a small structure on a flat roof, or provided that the site is reasonably sunny, where the garden is little more than a backyard and too small to 'lay out' for either flowerbeds or kitchen garden.

The building, equipment, and maintenance of the older solidly built greenhouses was an expensive business until recent years. Lighter modern methods of construction, particularly the use of light metal, and the development of portable houses built in sections, have gone far towards making greenhouse ownership popular. While it may not be a necessity, a greenhouse is none the less a very valuable asset to the amateur gardener.

1. It permits the enjoyment of plants throughout the year and is especially valuable in winter when gardening out of doors is difficult.

2. It enables the gardener to raise both vegetable and flower seedlings weeks earlier than in the open garden and to plant them well advanced when weather conditions allow.

3. It is particularly valuable to those who find that bending and stooping on routine garden operations are no longer so easy. They can sit on a stool and prick out or carry out similar operations in warm and congenial conditions.

The question of how best to utilize the greenhouse depends largely on the interests, taste, and inclination of its owner. The one thing he should not do is to attempt to do too much at once. He can undertake any of the following alternatives:

1. Use it as a mixed house, growing a few plants each of whatever genera he is most interested in; for example, pelargoniums, begonias, fuchsias, etc.

2. He can use it largely for overwintering tender plants (either indoor plants or bedding material for the adornment of the garden in the summer) and for propagation.

3. It may be used entirely for one genus such as carnations, or for a combination of two seasonal crops such as tomatoes in summer and chrysanthemums in autumn and winter.

4. It may be used for a group of plants requiring similar conditions for cultivation such as cacti and succulents.

5. It may be used to raise annual and biennial plants from seed, keeping up a succession of flowers over most of the year.

6. It can be devoted largely to what are termed 'house plants' for domestic use, giving these plants periods in the greenhouse between spells of duty in the house in order to keep them in good condition.

7. An unheated house can be utilized for alpine plants, or for gently bringing along bulbs and flowering shrubs in pots.

The term 'greenhouse' as used today covers all kinds of construction. Half a century ago special types of house all had their own names and uses. The one given most heat was known as the stove. It had a rigid minimum of 60°F. and woe betide the stoker who allowed the thermometer to drop below. This was of course used for tropical plants. Houses in which temperatures of 55°F. to 60°F. were maintained were known as intermediate or temperate houses, and so on. Below these were cool houses and conservatories in which plants were staged while in flower, for it is well known that most plants will remain a great deal longer in flower under cool airy conditions than in greater heat and humidity. Special houses were designed for orchids, and there were Palm Houses, Vineries, Peach Houses, etc., each for its own particular purpose.

The term 'cold house' does not imply refrigeration, but merely that no artificial heat is normally given, though frequently a paraffin or electric heater is used during frost, sometimes in conjunction with blinds on the outside.

The day of such ranges has of course gone! The high, and still rising, cost of fuel prohibits high temperatures. Today is then the era of the cool greenhouse, in which the cost of heating is kept to a minimum and which for, say, seven months of the year is not heated at all.

While some genera or groups of plants require specialized conditions, for example full sunlight in the case of succulents and cacti, high humidity for many orchids, etc., a very good number of plants are still sufficiently easy going and adaptable to get along under the same general conditions, and it is really astonishing what a range of material can be grown without artificial heat for seven or eight months of the year, and for the remaining four or five only requires protection from frost. For this purpose 45°F. is a safe minimum though a drop to 40°F. in very severe weather will do no great harm if the plants are dry at the roots. For some of these plants those whose gardens are in coastal regions or in sheltered parts of the West Country will need no greenhouse, whereas those in bleak areas of the Midlands and North must provide some form of protection – the comfortable warmth of a greenhouse being, of course, the best. For the purposes of this book we will define the cool greenhouse as one with a minimum temperature of, say, 45° F. and an average of, say, 60° F., while with most plants, though not all, no great harm is done if *sun* heat pushes it up to 80° F. or over. Sections on succulent plants, on foliage plants for the house, and on the Alpine house have been left out of this book, since these subjects will be covered more fully by separate volumes to be published later in this series. Brief sections only have been included on carnations and chrysanthemums, since these also will be dealt with later in other volumes. They are, however, strictly cool greenhouse plants in many cases.

1 · Constructing, Equipping, and Heating the Greenhouse

Constructing the Greenhouse

SITUATION AND ASPECT. Apart from the small prefabricated houses the building of glass structures generally is a highly specialized form of construction. There are a number of firms who have built up a reputation for design and quality of workmanship over several generations and can be relied upon whatever type of material is used. For any building which involves problems of siting, difficult levels, or unusual design, they are the people best qualified to advise.

An important point with either greenhouses or frames is that a brick or concrete permanent structure cannot as a rule be removed by a tenant. Even with a portable or sectional type of greenhouse it is as well to have a written agreement with the landlord before building. It should also be moved before and not after the tenancy ceases.

Another preliminary is to discuss the question with the local authorities. They can stop building on to a dwelling house or other structure, particularly if this is likely to interfere with ventilation.

The most essential point in choosing a suitable site in Britain is full sunshine. Shelter from north and east too will make a vast difference in the amount of heating necessary. Greenhouses are generally built to run north and south. In *Science and the Glasshouse* the question of orientation is studied and the author, Mr W. J. C. Lawrence, points out that an east to west house is very much better for winter light and therefore particularly valuable for winter propagation.

There are several points which must be considered before placing the house in position. Full sunshine is essential, so shade from nearby buildings or trees must be avoided so far as possible. In a wet situation drainage may be required, or a layer of clinker or ashes laid to raise the site. The best foundation is, of course, a concrete floor with a layer of bricks to take the house where it is glazed to ground level, or a brick wall for the bench type.

1. A typical small span roof with both side and top ventilation. The brick built frames are valuable, particularly for 'hardening off' plants before planting out.

PERMANENT CONSTRUCTION. For a permanent house without a centre staging 9 to 11 feet is a convenient width. This allows 3 feet for a path and 3 to 4 feet each for the benches. If a centre stage is required with a path round it, it should not be less than 16 to 18 feet wide. Length is to a considerable extent more flexible and it may be desirable and more economic to build a long structure partitioned to provide two sets of growing conditions, temperatures, etc. (Plate 1).

The limitations apart from cost are possible difficulties of siting and the fact that with boiler heating the pipes must rise from the boilers to the extreme end if effective circulation is to be ensured.

There are three main types of greenhouse construction, though for specialized purposes they are modified as required.

The commonest and for most purposes the most useful is the span roofed house. It is built like a barn usually with roof sides equal in length. Proportions vary tremendously from the tiny 8 by 12 feet to commercial houses covering huge areas. A recently developed modified form of span roof house is based on the work

2. A smaller structure of the lean-to type, of all-metal construction.

of Mr W. J. C. Lawrence at the John Innes Institution. This has the two sides sloping at different angles in order to take full advantage of winter light.

The three-quarter span or hip span usually utilizes a wall, say 8 or 10 feet in height, and has a short span at the back on the wall side and a longer sloping side on the other. It should face south to receive full light and sun, although there are exceptions; for example, a fernery is usually placed on the north or shady side. Though not so popular today, this kind of house was widely used particularly for vines and peaches in the days of large private gardens. Used as a plant house it is usually fitted with staging to bring the plants at the back nearer the roof glass; this, properly placed, is the best type of house for winter, particularly if the back wall is whitewashed, or as suggested by Mr Lawrence, tiled, to give maximum reflection of light.

The cheapest form of permanent house is the lean-to, using a wall of 8 or 10 feet as the back and a sloping roof of one side only Plate 2). A sunny situation is essential for this. The wall at the

3. The greenhouse made of Alumabrite and exhibited in *The Times* Garden of Tomorrow at the Chelsea Show 1959. The Vent-Axia fan for automatic ventilation can be seen at the end of the house above the door. The house is shaded automatically by water containing a dye being re-circulated over the glass. Rod thermostats can be seen at each side of the house below the glass and the control panel for the house is on the left of the door. On the right of the plants is a bench for propagation under mist and in the nearer part of the bench is automatic watering controlled by electricity. The tomatoes on the left have soil heating and there is illumination from the lights along the top.

back tends to absorb heat during the hours of sunny weather and this heat is radiated at night. It also, of course, reduces the chilling effects of north winds. One of the main drawbacks of this kind of house is that it usually only has ventilators on the front, and should the wind be from this direction it is difficult to avoid draughts which can have serious results. The use of up-to-date fan ventilation would get over this difficulty. The blocking of light on the wall side also tends to cause plants to grow towards the light. For tenants' fixtures they should not be built into the wall but rest on a plate or lead flushing on the wall which remains when the structure is removed.

Forcing pits are usually quite low structures like frames of the span roof type but without (or at any rate very low) vertical walls. They may either have the lights hinged for access or they may have a narrow path sunk through the centre of the house to allow the gardener to stand erect. No staging is used in this type of structure, the plants being grown on ashes or gravel at ground level. They are largely used commercially for ferns and similar kinds of pot plant and on a large scale for cucumbers and melons. They were at one time very extensively used in private gardens, but are now largely superseded by modern metal frames or Dutch Light structures.

Dutch Lights are simply large panes of glass of standard size contained in a wooden frame. They are used for both houses and frames. For the former a framework is erected, of wood, metal, or concrete, to take these lights, usually two at the sides and two forming a span for the roof. For commercial houses they are used in a big way. The advantages are, first, that they are cheaper than orthodox construction, and length can be extended as required. Secondly, they can readily be moved to a new site. Thirdly, the large panes of glass give maximum light at top and sides. If desired, heating equipment may be installed using portable boilers and easily fitted hot-water pipes. Both houses and frames are primarily built to grow plants in the soil, but they are adaptable, and may be used for seedlings in boxes, for hardening off both bedding plants and vegetable seedlings, and of course for pot plants.

PREFABRICATED CONSTRUCTION. With the passing of the ranges of the old private garden has come both a radical change in greenhouse design and a wider choice of materials. Until recent years wood has always been the material used and has indeed certain advantages, particularly low initial cost and suitability for the amateur craftsman. The cost of maintenance and repair today, however, is pricing the orthodox type of construction off the market. The cost of painting in particular is continually rising. With small houses, however, where the amateur can deal with the problem himself, the cost is often lower than with other materials. There are now on the market a number of timbers which do not require painting, though they most probably will require oiling occasionally with linseed oil. There is also a method of protecting roof bars by a metal alloy capping which should appreciably prolong the life of the greenhouse, or an alternative method uses waterproof tape to cover the bars (Plate 4). There are also chemical wood preservatives. The design of timber construction

4. Using a waterproof tape to protect or repair defective glazing.

is today much lighter than it was before the war. Wider panes admit more light, and ventilating gear, gutters, etc., are all of lighter construction for the same reason. Too flimsy construction must, however, be avoided as wind can cause vibration and breakages; and snow, if heavy, can also cause damage. The main bearers should also be strong enough to take the weight of maintenance work, reglazing, painting, etc.

A visit to one of the large flower shows such as The Royal Horticultural Society's Chelsea Show is probably the best way to select the type of house most suitable to one's purpose and pocket. They are shown in greater range and diversity year by year, in timber, metal, and concrete. Timber construction may be in softwoods such as Western Red Cedar, in teak, and in the newer hardwoods which do not require painting, or in oak. Design and size vary considerably within a wide range of prices.

Side by side with these are structures of aluminium and steel, again in a considerable range of sizes and prices. Here also are houses built of concrete which can be supplied ready-made and erected on your own footings. Not only should the structures be studied carefully but also the benches, shelves, and equipment generally, not forgetting different methods of heating. The type of door is important, particularly with metal houses, where the sliding kind are very much better than the hinged, which are always giving trouble, particularly in windy weather.

It is not always desirable to go for the minimum sizes; slightly larger structures cost relatively little more and give infinitely more pleasure in working than the more cramped conditions of the tiniest. Erection of a larger size is no more difficult, nor does it take much longer.

Teak is probably still the best timber for greenhouses, with its long life, but will be too costly for most people. Oak is being used to some extent (Plate 5). It is undoubtedly the best of the British timbers, but is somewhat inclined to warp unless very well seasoned. Several imported hardwoods have been tried in recent years as substitutes for teak. These seem to promise well, but they have not been long enough in use for comparisons to be made as regards durability. Softwoods often used in addition to Western Red Cedar (not really a cedar), are Scots Pine and Baltic Redwood.

Construction in light metal alloys has most certainly come to stay. There is far less obstruction of light than with either timber or concrete, and though more expensive, they have a long

5. Span roof greenhouse built of oak with wire strengthening.

6. Metal house on brick base, designed for bench cultivation.

7. Metal house, glass to ground, used for both chrysanthemums and smaller pot plants on staging; both this and the house in Plate 6 are 10 feet wide, 7 feet 1 inch high, and 12 feet 5 inches long.

potential life (Plates 6 and 7). The materials are treated before erection so that they should not need painting. The glass is fixed by new plastic compounds which do not crack and come away as putty sometimes does, and which reduce breakages by structural movement. Some of the newer types are built of aluminium alloy in arches of lattice work without any post or other obstruction, and with large panes of glass which admit the maximum possible amount of light. A number of different designs and makes are available, some quite small, and there is no doubt that once the initial cost is met, maintenance is light. The smooth surface of aluminium affords no foothold for insect pests, nor is it suitable for the development or spread of fungoid troubles. In many designs the drip due to condensation is avoided by grooves or channels to carry away the moisture.

Steel-built houses have the advantages of strength and durability, and the initial cost is usually considerably less than with aluminium alloys. The better quality makes are of rolled steel, rust-proofed by galvanizing. They are glazed in much the same way as are aluminium houses, using a pliable plastic material instead of putty. The narrow steel frames allow in the maximum light, they are easily put together, and look a neat finished job. Provision is often made in the frames for the fixing of shelves, as in Plate 6. The cheaper types of steel houses sometimes offered are not to be recommended as they must be painted frequently and, once erected, there are corners not easy to reach with a paint brush.

Concrete houses of the prefabricated type have the advantages that they are easily erected and need no preservative painting or other maintenance (Plate 8). The fabric cannot rot as timber does and, for those who live near the sea, it is not affected by salt-laden winds. The glass is securely fixed by plastic putty, and on erection the bearers are painted with a special white paint which lasts for some years and gives excellent light reflection. It is also claimed for these houses that they retain heat better than do other materials.

Houses are built specially for the amateur in all these materials. Many of them are essentially tenant fixtures and easily dismantled and re-erected. A recent development which may have far-

8. A strongly built house of concrete construction.

reaching results is a greenhouse built of plastic materials over a timber or metal framework. Time alone will tell to what extent these will stand up to climatic conditions, particularly strong sunshine. I have not yet had an opportunity of seeing one. Another type is evidently in use in America under the name of Fiber Glass Houses.

Equipping the Greenhouse

An important point to be settled when planning the greenhouse is whether or not to have benches. It is very largely a question of what is to be grown, and also depends on the design of the house. If it is built on a brick, timber, or concrete wall 2 or 3 feet in height, a stage or bench is undoubtedly necessary. With houses glazed to the ground they may not be required. Except for tomato or vegetable cultivation, however, benches are usually preferable. They bring one's plants up to eye level, usually provide better control of moisture, and are certainly warmer in winter. A convenient width of bench for a small house is from 3 to 4 feet.

They may be of several different materials. For the larger types of house the cheapest in the long run are concrete benches with a

9. Greenhouse with annuals showing the staging and pea gravel.

good strong verge. There is nothing better than slate if it can be obtained locally, but its cost and transport rule it out for most localities.

The reason for the verge is that a good deep layer of shingle or pea gravel on the bench will hold moisture and is the best insurance against pots being completely dried out during the owner's absence (Plate 9). This is the worst objection to the open slat type of stage. Another is that small pots are always being knocked over. Small houses are usually fitted with these slats, either in wood or aluminium. For the latter it is worth while having zinc trays made to fit them, in which small plants may be plunged. Even small succulents are far less trouble plunged in this way. Before doing so, however, make sure that the structure is strong enough to take the increased weight. Other alternatives to the wooden slats are corrugated iron sheets, or, more long-lasting, asbestos sheets. For large structures, however, the most permanent and serviceable job is prefabricated concrete. A point which must be kept in mind is that there must be a gap at the back of the stage for the warmed air to rise.

Where hot-water heating is to be used, the boiler should be at the north end of a north to south house, so that light is not

27

obstructed by boiler, chimney, or fuel, and perhaps more important, the smoke is likely to be carried away by west, south-west, or even east winds. To have the chimney on the side of the prevailing winds means constant cleaning of the glass. Should the house run east to west, the boiler would be best at the east end.

Whatever type of heating installation is to be used some kind of propagating case should be included. Some of the rustless metal frames made for the purpose are excellent. Small electrically heated cases are also made and the benches may, if desired, be warmed by soil heating wires. This will allow a lower minimum air temperature to be maintained and where thermostatic control is used would for most purposes prove economical.

Efficient ventilation is vital in a greenhouse and is the weak point in many of the small prefabricated houses. The manually operated sash will probably soon be a thing of the past, for it means that someone must always be available to deal with climatic changes. Where it is used it must be controlled by worm and wheel mechanism. Automatic ventilation, thermostatically controlled, will alter this completely, not only being more accurate but also more economical in that the ventilators will close as the temperature falls, not after. While still in the experimental stage, it is probable that vents along the ridge of the roof and at the base of the house will replace the conventional gear which causes a good deal of obstruction to light. Vents of this kind containing exhaust fans will avoid the need for sashes and eliminate draughts due to wind changes, etc. One is shown in Plate 13.

Paths should be of solid construction. While concrete is largely used, there is a great deal to be said for the patterned bricks which were made for the purpose. The pattern held a certain amount of water and the bricks themselves were of an absorbent nature. The width of the path to a great extent depends on the size of the house. A wide house is relatively more economical than a narrow one, since the path need not necessarily be wider. For small houses 3 feet·is convenient and 2 feet a rather cramped minimum.

Another point to be borne in mind before building is the desirability of conserving rain-water. Hard water is disliked by many plants and though mains water must be provided, or some other copious source, it is worth while sinking a galvanized iron tank and collecting rain-water from the gutters, an overflow must also be provided to take surplus water to the drains.

GARDEN FRAMES. Whether heated or not, frames can be extremely valuable, either independently of the greenhouse, or, better still, complementary to it. A number of exotic plants are happier grown cold until weather conditions make it necessary to move them indoors. Cold frames are valuable also for hardening off seedlings, bedding plants, etc., and in many other ways.

Many types of frames are now on the market, some of the most elaborate construction. In its simplest form a frame is a structure of brick, wood, concrete, or metal, on which the lights – glass or glass substitute in a light framework of wood or metal – are rested. They keep the plants snug and allow the maximum light to reach them. Ventilation can be adjusted as required. The older permanent type of frame was usually made for 6- by 4-foot lights in series of twos, fours, or more. These are capacious, but they do tend to be heavy to work, and for this reason smaller sizes, 4 by 4 feet 6 inches (or 4 feet 2 inches square) have now become popular. There are also, as previously noted, the Dutch Light structures.

For general purposes frames are built to slope from back to front, allowing rain to drain off freely, and sited to face south as nearly as possible. It is often possible to incorporate a row of frames alongside a permanent greenhouse (Plate 1). This gives them both shelter and warmth through the wall. In this case the lights are better hinged at the back for access.

Another design is the span-roofed frame, which is in fact a miniature greenhouse. Here the light is hinged to the centre and the frame is deep enough to accommodate quite tall plants.

Both softwoods and the newer hardwoods which require no painting are now widely used for frames. Owing to the recent scarcity and poor quality of timber, however, and the development of prefabricated concrete, this new material is fast replacing the old. It gives first-class protection, and should last a lifetime. The frames are made in sections which are bolted together, so

10. A metal frame. This can be used either out of doors or as a propagating case under glass. They are strong, durable, and rustless.

although heavy they are still mobile. The lights are of course wood and glass, and of standard, interchangeable, sizes 6 by 4 feet and 4 by 3 feet.

Metal frames are now available in a bewildering range of design and size. Those made in rustless metal are excellent value, easy to move about and to ventilate (Plate 10).

Heating Methods

To maintain an adequate temperature in the greenhouse is not quite so easy as it may seem. There are a number of factors to consider. Heat losses will vary with the type and construction of the house and with its aspect, whether sheltered or exposed. The greatest loss is usually through the laps of the glass and cracked and defective panes. Heat is lost also to a certain extent through floor, soil, brickwork, and perhaps more especially through ventilators. The loss of heat also differs in different forms of construction. Steel, for instance, loses much more heat than wood. All these factors are well known to the heating engineer and the first thing he does is to estimate the number of B.T.U.s (British

Thermal Units) required to make good this heat loss, for each Fahrenheit degree the interior temperature exceeds the external. He then has to estimate the heating required to raise the temperature of the house one Fahrenheit degree. From these figures he can work out the B.T.U.s required to keep the temperature inside to a safe degree when the thermometer outside registers perhaps 20° F. of frost.

There is nowadays a wide choice in the method of heating, though this must to some extent depend on locality. For a large installation the traditional hot-water system is still probably the most economic. For smaller outfits the advantages of electricity may outweigh its probably higher cost.

What is required by the amateur is a sufficient heating surface to keep out frost without making too much demand on his time in stoking night and morning. For this purpose the piping should not be skimped.

It is much better to have a large heating surface warm, rather than a shorter one excessively hot. The latter is bad both for the plants and for the boiler which often has to be driven hard in bad weather. With hot-water heating there is now a much greater range in the choice of fuel. Coal and coke can be supplied in special grades to suit the type of boiler; many boilers are adapted for oil fuel and some for gas.

For large greenhouses heating by hot-water circulation has many advantages providing the piping is adequate. The warmth produced is neither too fierce nor too drying in its effect. The usual method is to utilize the principle that hot water rises and cold water falls. The piping is so arranged that the highest part of the circulation system is farthest from the boiler, and a return pipe below brings back the colder water to the boiler. It has always been thought that 4-inch pipes were best for keeping an even degree of heating, but some modern installations are being done with 2-inch pipes more frequently spaced. A rise as little as 1 inch in 10 feet will give a circulation provided that it is a steady rise, but the steeper the rise the more rapid will be the movement of the water. Where it is not possible to sink the boiler, an overhead suspension of the pipes may be necessary.

Boilers of many different types and sizes are obtainable, the smaller designs being simply a water jacket similar to the domestic hot-water system. In the larger types, however, the water passes through spaces at the sides and top of the firebox and thus is heated as well by the hot flue gases as they pass through to the chimney.

Modern boilers are capable of burning many hours without attention. In some, a self-feeding apparatus or feed hopper is fitted so that as fuel is consumed fresh fuel is fed to the fire. For this purpose special grades are essential. A further refinement is in the shaking grates which get rid of ashes without the strenuous use of pokers and rakes. They can also be fitted with an automatic damper controlled by a thermostat usually working from the return water-pipe.

Some makes of small boilers are built into the brickwork of the end of the house. Others stand a foot or so away, the pipes passing through the brickwork. The chimney for these, usually a metal pipe, is fixed by metal supports to the house. With larger installations, however, a brick chimney is necessary and the boilers are usually sunk below greenhouse level and roofed over. Protected in this way from wind and weather, the boiler is more easily controlled and firing a great deal more congenial in bad weather. Efficient lagging (that is, covering the pipes with non-conducting material) is necessary for all exposed pipes outside the greenhouse. The efficient working of the boiler depends largely on 'draught' and the height of the chimney must be sufficient to ensure this.

CHOICE OF FUEL. Before deciding on the type of heating to be adopted, the fuels available and their relative cost must be carefully considered. It was at one time usual to use coke almost exclusively, but this has increased in cost so much that at the moment better results are obtained at less cost by using anthracite coal. However, relative costs may change again. These will also vary with transport costs according to locality, so that it is unwise to dogmatize. The best advice one can give is to consult a good heating engineer who is familiar with your own local conditions of supply.

Automatic stoking is now being used extensively for larger

boilers, and where thermostatically controlled they avoid all the drudgery and dirt normally associated with stoking. This method involves special types of fuel, and should supplies be cut it can be difficult to save the situation. Such outfits are extremely expensive to install, but they do save a tremendous amount of dirty, strenuous labour. They should always be installed by a competent heating engineer, as faults or defects may prove not only exasperating but costly.

For large boilers oil fuel is now being extensively used and, provided the right grade is easily obtainable, it has several advantages. It is clean to use, easier and less bulky to store, and properly burned gives less smoke and dirt than most solid fuels. The heating installation can remain without alteration, but the fire bars are replaced by fire bricks and jets or nozzles used in which air is mixed with the vaporized oil in much the same way as with a blow-lamp. The air is fed in by a compressor driven by an electric motor. Control of fuel and air (and consequently size of flame) is by thermostat in the greenhouse, giving automatic control of greenhouse temperatures.

Gas heating never seems to have been much used in horticulture. This may be due to the knowledge that gas fumes can be deadly to plant life. It is an efficient means of heating and used in a stokehole well away from the greenhouses might prove cheaper than some other forms of heating. It would be thermostatically controlled, is clean and easy to use, there is no wastage, and it is of course labour-saving. It would obviously have to be installed by competent workmen from the Gas Company or makers. It is vital that there should be no leakage of gas into the house, and the chimney must be of sound construction and sufficient height to keep fumes from the house. A small boiler specially designed for heating the greenhouse is now manufactured and is sponsored by the Gas Boards.

For small houses, particularly those with a low minimum temperature, there are specially made paraffin heaters of varied design. Those fitted with an external chimney and heating hot air tubes or water-pipes from which the heat is radiated, are the most satisfactory. The open flame type are only suitable for emergency use, as there is always danger of damage by fumes.

33

To avoid damage of this kind and also to provide the necessary oxygen for combustion a little ventilation is necessary. This at the same time keeps down the temperature and in consequence makes the method less efficient. Scrupulous cleanliness with the burners is also important.

ELECTRICAL HEATING. This has immense advantages. It is in fact said to be the complete answer for the busy man who is away from home most of the day. Temperature control is automatic and there is no morning and evening stoking. The thermostat ensures that no current is consumed at all when the temperature is above the control figure.

Before deciding what type of such heating to install I would advise the gardener to read a most useful book, *Electricity in the Garden*, by Geoffrey Gerard, in which the whole subject is covered without unnecessary technicalities.

The thermostat must be of an efficient type and it must be set and corrected, using a thermometer which is known to be accurate. It is a mistake to use equipment which is not made for the greenhouse. The most up-to-date type is the rod type fitted with a waterproof head (Plate 11). Designed and made for the purpose, it will stand high humidity and work within narrow limits. It must be fixed horizontally, screened from direct sunshine, and a foot or so away from the glass. It must also, of course, be right away from heaters of any kind.

The method of electrical heating most used today is the tubular heater – hollow aluminium tubes containing the heating element (Plate 12). They give a good distribution of heat, take up very little space, and are not difficult to fit. They are usually made for household voltage, burning 60 watts per foot run of tube, and are made in varying lengths, so that any reasonable loading can be made. They are fixed on brackets on the walls or on posts driven into the soil, preferably at least 6 inches away from the walls. A new development being used in some greenhouses is a fan heater (Plate 13), the air being blown by the fan over the heaters and into the house.

To convert an existing hot-water system to electrical heating, the boiler is replaced by a water tank, and an electric immersion

11. Rod type of thermostat recommended for greenhouse work.

12. Tubular heaters designed for greenhouse heating.

13. Fan heater being used in conjunction with fan ventilation.

heater similar to those used for the bath water is fitted. Still another type of immersion heater is made which can be fitted into the return pipes of an old hot-water system, either as an extra boost to the boiler or as an insurance against boiler failure.

There are also convector heaters made for the greenhouse in which air enters at the bottom, passes over a heating element, and out at the top. These must be placed in an open situation, never under the benches. They are said to give a dry heat and so to be not so good for successful cultivation.

The loading required is estimated in kilowatts (1000 watts), each producing 3412 B.T.U.s. Installation is best left in the hands of a competent electrical engineer, preferably one specializing in greenhouse heating, who will give a previous estimate of the cost. Accurate estimation of the consumption required is difficult. Assuming that the thermostat is set at 50° F., the heaters will cut out with every burst of sunshine, so that in all but severe weather consumption will depend on locality and the frequency and power of the sunshine. A most important point when estimating the heating requirements is to allow sufficient power to cover a fall to 20° below freezing-point.

The growth of plants is dependent also on the soil temperature, and this is now receiving much more attention than formerly. It is claimed that with a soil temperature of 60° F. in a greenhouse floor or bench, the air temperature may be allowed to drop to 45° F. for most plants normally cultivated by the amateur.

For soil warming, the voltage is usually cut down to 8 or 12 volts and the current passed through naked wire buried in the soil (Plate 14). For propagating frames and benches, these are buried in 5 or 6 inches of sand. For borders they are sunk more deeply, about 9 inches deep, to allow surface cultivation. The wires heat to 110° F., the warmth diffusing through the sand. For propagation purposes the seed pots and pans, and subsequently the seedlings, are rested or partly sunk in the warmed sand. To conserve as much heat as possible, granulated peat is worked through between the pots, or they can be plunged into the peat as they are put in place. An alternative method is to use mains voltage, but in this case the cable is made in fixed loads and insulated. It must not be cut or interfered with. The latter method

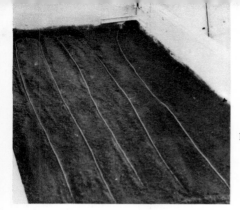

14. Soil-warming cables on a propagating bench ready for covering with sand or peat.

is cheaper to install because of the cost of the transformer in the other.

The one great risk with electricity is, of course, that power cut or failure during severe weather can be disastrous.

It seems unnecessary to stress that greenhouse heating can be an expensive business and that very careful consideration should be given to the choice of installation. It is obviously better to spend a little extra on initial cost on really efficient apparatus, rather than make do perhaps for years with something second-rate.

15. A Dutch Light frame heated by soil-warming, and also air-warmed by cables which are controlled by a rod-type thermostat.

2 · The Potting Shed

General Considerations

Though not absolutely necessary, the provision of some kind of potting shed is most desirable. If the potting and handling of one's plants has to be done in the greenhouse, not only is a good deal of valuable space wasted but it is difficult to keep the house clean and tidy. It soon becomes cluttered up with pots and pans, staking and tying materials, and soil is trodden all over the floor.

A well-equipped shed soon pays its way and provides storage for garden tools, insecticides, fungicides, fertilizers, and the hundred and one commodities which some time or another will find their way into the garden. It should be as close as possible to the greenhouse to avoid having tender unestablished plants and seedlings in the open air longer than is necessary, and it should if possible be on the same level. A reasonable amount of head room is desirable, otherwise tall plants cannot be handled on the potting bench, and a window at the side of the bench will facilitate the handling of small seedlings. If this is difficult a skylight may be fitted, and if possible electric light for evening working. It is quite a good practice to combine the shed with a small boiler to heat the greenhouse and incidentally to keep the shed warm. The bench itself should be a solid job, preferably of 1½-inch timber – nothing is more annoying than a bench which bounces when potting! It should be a convenient height for comfortable working, say 3 feet 6 inches high, and wide enough to hold a reasonable volume of potting soil, pots, etc.; 4 feet is not too wide.

A small portable potting bench in the form of a tray is also useful and enables light jobs such as pricking out seedlings to be done in the greenhouse if, for example, it is too cold to work comfortably in the shed. It can also be used out of doors in fine weather if placed on a trestle or suitable box. A convenient size is 4 by 3 feet sides and back 9 to 12 inches high. It will also be found of value for labelling purposes, as it can be used wherever required.

Under the bench will usually be the best place to store potting materials, or prepared compost. The latter should be kept in a dust-bin or similar receptable to avoid contact with unsterilized material, and the entry of fungus spores, weed seeds, etc.

Another essential is a well-made pot rack which will keep pots and pans tidy, and which will quickly save its costs in breakages. Its size must of course be relative to the size of the shed, and the greenhouse, but it is always best to have the deeper shelves at the base to accommodate large and heavy pots, placing the smaller sizes on the higher shelves. Pots must always be laid horizontally. Standing one inside the other vertically in piles causes cracking and breakages.

Pots are sold by the potter's 'cast'. Depending on size and thickness of the pot, he can get one very large pot (a No. 1) or up to 72 small ones from the same volume of clay. The smallest are called 72's and the others generally used are 60's, i.e. $2\frac{1}{2}$ inches in diameter, 48's, $4\frac{1}{2}$ inches in diameter by 5 inches deep and usually known as 5-inch pots, 32's and 24's. They should not be glazed.

SIZES OF POTS

	Diameter inside pot at top, in inches
72	2
60	$2\frac{1}{2}$
48	$4\frac{1}{2}$
32	6
24	$8\frac{1}{2}$
16	$9\frac{1}{2}$
12	$11\frac{1}{2}$
8	12
6	13
4	15
2	18

There is also an extensive range of the shallow receptacles called pans available, both round and rectangular. The round type are extensively used for ferns and succulents. They are also useful for plants at the edge of the stagings which are apt to be knocked off. They are equally valuable for bulbs which are being forced and after flowering either planted out or discarded, and which therefore will not be long in the pans. The rectangular (or square) type are most useful for pricking out seedlings, especially slow-growing ones like *Lilium*. They fit in together snugly whereas with the round ones there is always a certain waste of space.

The first thing to do after buying new pots or pans is to put them into a tank or bucket of water and leave them to soak for half an hour. Then drain and put away in the shed. If this is not done they will absorb the moisture from the potting compost when used. Before re-use old pots should be scrubbed to get rid of soil inside, and moulds, etc., outside. Both would prevent movement of air through the pot and, if a plant is put into a dirty pot, it will be found later that it is difficult to knock out the ball without damage to the roots. Even more important is the risk of transferring pests or diseases if dirty pots are re-used.

Tools and Equipment

The essential tools are few but should be of good design and quality, particularly the spade and shovel necessary in mixing soils; a good trowel is desirable and a strong knife or secateurs.

Staking and tying materials should also be to hand. Thin bamboo canes are still probably the most serviceable support for most pot plants, they are extremely strong yet not too conspicuous and ugly. There are all kinds of gadgets and wire contraptions on the market for the purpose. Many of them are no doubt efficient for their particular purposes, but they are usually not so adaptable to all kinds of plants and purpose.

Rammers are usually home-made. The larger sizes are easily made from a foot or so of broomstick, keeping one end an inch or so thick and rounded at the end, and tapering the other to a thin flat surface for working the soil down the side of the pots. With large pots it is difficult to work the soil down to the base with the fingers, though a sharp tap on the bench helps. A large wood label will serve the purpose well enough in an emergency. For seed receptacles the orthodox practice is to make rectangular and round pressers of $\frac{1}{2}$-inch board, a large one for pans and smaller round ones for pots; size depending on the pots generally used. A handle can be fitted by nailing through the board.

For those who make up their own composts two or three sieves are necessary for the screening of the loam, etc. Where composts are obtained prepared, sieves are less important, though they are useful for screening broken pots for drainage, and for the transport from place to place of small pots.

The size of mesh most generally used in the potting shed is the $\frac{1}{2}$ inch: a finer one is useful when seed sowing, and for this purpose $\frac{1}{4}$ inch is most suitable. Some gardeners also use a fine wire mesh like a flour sieve, for distributing sand evenly over seed pots after sowing.

Labelling

In any collection of plants some method of labelling is desirable. In a small private collection and particularly with perennial plants it saves time and labour to buy ready numbered labels and simply enter new plants as received under this number in a note-book. With plants which are propagated annually such as chrysanthemums or pelargoniums, labelling is essential, as out of flower it is all too easy to get stocks mixed up, and perhaps propagate wrong varieties.

The next question is what kind of labels are most suitable and economical. There are three main types, wood, metal, and plastic. The old-fashioned wooden 'tallies' which have been used for generations have several disadvantages. For the writing to remain legible for any length of time they must be painted and the writing done while the paint is still wet. This preserves the name but the end in the soil is liable to rot away until the label has to be discarded. Many ways of postponing this have been used, probably the best being to soak the ends in copper napthanate and then to dry thoroughly before using. Creosote is not recommended, but there are similar proprietary materials which are advertised as safe and effective. It was for the same reason that the custom of always writing the name from the top (square end) of the label arose; if the 'soil end' rotted the name was usually still legible.

This is the day of metal alloys and in labelling these have made their mark as in other spheres. Aluminium alloys have the advantage of being almost indestructible, they are neat and easy to write with soft lead pencils or indian ink. They are also made so that they can be attached to or hung on the plant without additional ties, and a fair range of size is available. Embossed labels of zinc are even more durable though the names have to be punched by machine. Stamped lead labels also are available with blank labels which one can print with a handy little machine, or the list of names may be submitted and the labels obtained ready printed.

Plastics also have come to stay and in many collections, particularly of orchids, succulents, and cacti, they are used exclusively. The material called xylonite is perhaps most popular. It can be obtained in sheets and cut to any size desired, and is durable, and the resulting labels can be neat and legible. It has another great advantage in that the label may be made triangular and the name written horizontally, which avoids many a pain in the neck! Many other kinds have been tried or are on trial, but for the amateur the aluminium alloy and plastic types are probably the handiest and most convenient.

Potting

Even the potting shed has its own terminology and, as it is reasonably stable in horticultural books and the Press, we had better define what is meant.

PRICKING OFF is the first stage; it simply means the initial transfer from the pot or pan in which seed is germinated, to pots (or boxes) in which they are to be grown on.

It is best done at the earliest possible moment after germination, that is, as early as the seedling can be conveniently handled. Experiment has proved that there is less shock to the seedlings in their earliest stages than later, when they have made some root. The roots are unavoidably damaged in the transfer, with a consequent check to the seedling.

16. Potting off young gloxinias from the box in which they have been started into growth.

POTTING OFF. This applies more in commercial work where seedlings are first boxed and then transferred to pots (Plate 16). It is only justified on the grounds of saving space and where possible should be avoided (see *Science and the Glasshouse*, by W. J. C. Lawrence).

POTTING ON implies the moving on of seedlings already in pots into larger sizes. This should be done as soon as the roots are running freely round the pot and before the young plant becomes what is called potbound (Plates 17 and 18).

The experimental work at John Innes Institute proves that plants may safely be given a larger pot than was generally practised provided J.I. composts are used (Plate 19).

RE-POTTING may be again potting these on, but more often means the annual overhaul of perennial plants. Whether the size of pot is increased or not depends on the kind of plant and its general condition.

17. Potting on cinerarias: the preparation of the pots by crocking to ensure efficient drainage.

18. Knocking out the young plant from the 60 pot.

19. Placing the plant in the 48 pot and firming the new compost round it.

CROCKING is a means of securing efficient drainage by means of pieces of broken pots or similar material placed at the bottom of pots. It is good sound practice to place an inverted 'crock', that is, a piece of broken pot hollow side down, over the drainage hole of the pot and a small handful of finely broken pots over and round it. By this means free drainage for a considerable period is ensured.

Next, it is wise to put in some rough material, fibrous peat, loam fibre, or similar material if available, to prevent the compost working into the drainage. Failing this, use a handful of the roughest of the compost first.

We have recently been told that this method of drainage is out of date, costly, and unnecessary. For commercial purposes, where thousands of pots are being handled, and handled by experienced staff, that may well be so, but for those without that experience the old-fashioned practice is the safe one. A new dodge which may prove to be of value is to make pots with slots in the base of the pot sides to give improved drainage.

Potting. The actual procedure of potting is simple enough. Having prepared the drainage and a little roughage in the new pot, the plant to be potted is knocked out of its pot by turning upside down and tapping the edge of the pot on the bench (Plate 20). With the fingers of one hand holding the top of the ball and the other hand the pot, the edge of the pot is then tapped smartly until the plant slides out. Take out the old drainage crocks and place them to one side for washing and re-use. Next, add a little new compost and place the plant in the new pot and test it for depth. This should place the old collar (or top of the ball) about the same relative height as before; never deeper. If it seems too high, tease a little soil off the bottom of the ball; if too low, add a little more soil in the new pot bottom. This is important, as with many plants inserting too deeply will cause casualties, usually by rotting at the collar. Next, work a little soil down the sides of the ball and see that it is firm all the way to the drainage (Plate 21), using a rammer or wooden label to ensure this, and finally build up the soil to finished level. When working the soil into the pot, giving the plant a sharp tap or two on the bench will assist in working the soil down the sides of the pot and firming it. We have always been taught that the new compost should be as firm as the old ball or water would tend to run through it, leaving the old ball still dry (and don't forget you are depending on new root action from the old ball). Mr Lawrence, however (in *Science and the Glasshouse*), throws a spanner in the works and tells us that the rammer is on its way out and that the degree of firmness is not of major importance, but that the compost should be 'uniformly firmed to a moderate extent'.

Again it has always been a recognized practice not to move plants from a small into a very large pot at one move, but rather to pot on through successive stages from $2\frac{1}{2}$- to 5-inch to 7- to 9-inch as required. The motive here is partly to prevent sour, wet conditions which are not conducive to free root development.

Mr Lawrence asserts that with J.I. composts this is 'a shocking waste of labour' and that within reason the larger the pot the more rapid is the development of the young plants. He is of course writing primarily of commercial practice with plants such as tomatoes, but this method would apply equally to seedlings of

20. Knocking out a
    pot of rooted
    pelargoniums.

21. Potting off in size 60 pots.

such plants as calceolarias, schizanthus, and other greenhouse flowers, which if not moved on rapidly would show starvation. In commercial practice 'potting on' has been largely discarded, and tomatoes, for example, are moved from the seedling stage directly into fruiting sites. How far the amateur grower can follow this depends on the kinds of plant he is growing, but one thing is certain. If plants are given a large move, particular care must be given not to overwater.

One of the major difficulties with the novice is to decide how firmly to pot different types of plant, and it is one of those things which is extremely difficult to explain. Broadly speaking, it varies with the kind of growth. For example, a soft foliage plant like coleus requires little firming and definitely no hard ramming of the compost; on the other hand slow-growing woody plants such as palms should be rammed firmly with a wooden rammer. This rule also should be applied to size. For example, a young rooted cutting of chrysanthemum has soft and delicate roots and therefore requires gentle handling, merely firming with the fingers, while later in potting on, the new compost must be firm or later growth will tend to be soft. Another difficulty which requires some experience is to judge how much space below the rim to leave for watering; obviously if a pot is too full only a small volume of water can be applied and the danger is that the ball of soil may never be completely soaked, the plant suffering in consequence. Half an inch of rim should be left in sizes below 5-inch pots and at least an inch in larger sizes. It is general practice to keep plants on the dry side after potting, syringing, and shading if necessary to prevent flagging. This is done because in potting damage is done to the small roots and the fine root hairs which actually feed the plant; so that keeping the compost on the dry side prevents them rotting and aids the rapid recovery of the roots.

Plants will usually pass through the winter more safely if the pots are reasonably full of roots than they will if 'overpotted'. This condition is in fact one of the main causes of winter casualties, especially if it is coupled with too liberal use of the watering can, so with any plants which look well and show no signs of starvation, yellow foliage, for example, leave alone until early spring.

It must not be taken for granted that all kinds of plants must be continually moved into larger and larger pots. In fact the reverse is true; many thrive and flower better when in confined root room. I have known fuchsias, for example, in 6- or 7-inch pots for years, and remaining in fine condition. They are knocked out of the pots in early spring, and if the ball is in fair condition some of the old soil is teased off both top and sides of the ball and any dead roots cut away. The plant is then put back into a clean crocked pot of the same size and the new compost is worked in round the ball and firmed in with the potting rammer. If it is in vigorous health and justifies a move later on in the season, well and good. This method of potting is essential with many established perennial plants which will go several years without potting on. If one is continually moving them, lack of room soon becomes an acute problem. When potting these, by the way, cut out any dead wood and reduce straggly shoots so that top growth and root action can start together.

Composts

The term compost has more than one meaning in horticulture, but at the moment we are dealing with the ingredients which are to be used for the potting, or potting on, of plants.

At one time there were dozens of special mixtures recommended for various kinds of plants, in fact many gardeners had their own special composts, often closely guarded secrets. One of the most valuable pieces of research work ever carried out on practical horticulture was surely the standardizing of materials and the development of the now universally known John Innes Composts. This work was done at the John Innes Horticultural Institution (at Merton) by Messrs Lawrence and Newell and published in 1939 under the title *Seed and Potting Composts*.

By painstaking experiment and later by demonstration they proved that two basic composts could be used successfully for practically any kind of pot plant, and with minor modifications they are so used today. The prepared composts are now obtainable from most of the large horticultural sundries firms, made up to the J.I. formulae and steam sterilized. For a small garden and

49

greenhouse this can save a great deal of time, space, and trouble, apart from the fact that components obtainable locally may fall considerably below the high standard required.

The technique of steam (partial) sterilization of soils was worked out at the John Innes Institution as part of their research on soil composts. It is, of course, done to destroy disease spores and germs, eggs, and pupae of insects, and weed seeds in soil. The method is to heat the soil as quickly as possible to a temperature of 180°F. and hold it for ten minutes.

Growers who obtain the J.I. potting composts ready-made have no need to worry about sterilization of the soil, as this has already been done by steam. There are, however, several types of sterilizing outfits made for the small grower. The simplest is probably the kind using electricity in which a current passes through the soil which is heated by resistance to the passage of the current. There are also quite small models made for steam sterilizing, both fixed and portable, which are based on the original work at the John Innes Institution.

As a rule it is only necessary to sterilize the loam, but it is recommended that pots, pans, boxes, etc., also should be done. Sterilizing can be done by chemical means, but then some three or four weeks must elapse before the soil can be used. Formalin can be used at 1 part in 50 of water to 3 bushels of soil or cresylic acid 97 per cent purity at 1 in 40. The soil must be covered to retain the fumes for 48 hours.

JOHN INNES SEED COMPOST

			Superphosphate 1½ oz.	per bushel
			Chalk ¾ oz.	(8 gallons)
Parts	2 loam			
by	1 peat	+	OR	
bulk	1 sand			
			Superphosphate 2 lb.	per cubic
			Chalk 1 lb.	yard

JOHN INNES POTTING COMPOST

			J.I. base ¼ lb.	per bushel
			Chalk ¾ oz.	
Parts	7 loam			
by	3 peat	+	OR	
bulk	2 sand			
			J.I. base 5 lb.	per cubic
			Chalk 1 lb.	yard

The abbreviations used in connexion with these composts are:

J.I.S. for John Innes Seed Compost.

J.I.P.$_1$ for John Innes Potting Compost containing one dose of J.I. base and chalk.*

J.I.P.$_2$, the same compost but with a double dose of J.I. base and chalk.

J.I.P.$_3$, the same with a triple dose of J.I. base and chalk.

JOHN INNES BASE can be obtained ready-made from all sundriesmen who handle potting composts. The formula is:

Parts by	2 hoof and horn, ⅛ grist
weight	2 superphosphate of lime
	1 sulphate of potash

Loam is the most important ingredient in potting composts; it has been well defined as good soil in good condition. It is a mixture of sand, silt and clay in varying proportions; the relative amounts of sand and clay present making it 'light' and porous, or 'heavy' which implies a sticky condition difficult to work.

It is obtained from the turves cut from meadow or sometimes the surface of arable land, the former being most generally used. The turves are stacked until the grass and some of the roots are rotted. Coming as it does from all types of land it obviously must vary enormously in quality, and the essential thing when buying is to obtain it from a really reliable source.

Peat again varies a good deal, that from some districts being extremely acid; it serves to provide organic matter which rots and forms what is called 'humus' in the soil, helps to aerate the compost, and yet is retentive of moisture. When purchasing it is wise

* Chalk = ground chalk or limestone.

51

to ask for a special grade and stipulate that it is for use in J.I. composts. It is best stored under cover to avoid contamination by weed seeds, but before using must be spread out thinly and well moistened. In the case of baled peat the easy way is to make a hollow in one end and fill this basin repeatedly with water. It will expand and probably burst the bale. It must be evenly moistened before use.

Humus is a term widely used in horticulture. It is the product of the decomposition or breaking down of both plant and animal remains, largely by fungi and bacteria. It is usually dark brown or black in colour. In peat this breaking down has been slowed down or suspended by swampy conditions. It is in the provision of humus-forming material that the value of peat lies. Leaf mould is also a valuable source of humus, but it is very variable, depending on the kinds of leaves of which it is composed, its preparation, and storage.

Sand. For all potting purposes the coarser the grade of sand used the better. The main object is the drainage and porosity of the compost and fine sands are not so good. Sea sand is unsuitable as it may contain salt and lime in the form of crushed shells. Sands are easier to mix and handle if kept dry.

Fertilizers

No attempt will be made here to deal in detail with the extremely complex subject of the nutrients of plants. Sufficient to repeat that the essential nutrients needed in quantity by plants are nitrogen, phosphorus, and potash, and on many soils calcium also.

The first three together are known as a 'complete' fertilizer, the proportion of each being given as percentages of the total weight. While other elements are necessary they are only needed in minute amounts which are usually present in sufficient quantity in the compost. The term fertilizer in the broad sense means materials which are used as plant nutrients to supplement those already in the soil.

In the nitrogenous group the best known are the quick-acting inorganic sulphate of ammonia and nitrate of soda, both of which are extremely soluble in water. The latter is the most rapid in action and may be described as a plant tonic or pick-me-up. The effects are quickly seen in the colour of the foliage and more vigorous growth of the plant. To overdo it, however, results in soft sappy growth. Similar in action is dried blood. At the other and safer extreme is the slow-acting hoof and horn meal, an organic which is made by grinding the hoofs and horns of cattle. This is used in composts to give a steady result over a long period.

There are two groups of phosphatic fertilizers, those of organic origin and those known as inorganics. Bone meal is a slow-acting fertilizer made by grinding bones and extracting the fat. Steamed bone flour is very similar; both gradually disintegrate in the soil and release phosphoric acid. Superphosphate is made from insoluble rock phosphates chemically treated so that they become soluble in water. It is one of the best sources of phosphate. Basic slag is a by-product of the steel industry and is much more slow in action.

The fertilizer generally used as a supply of potash is sulphate of potash obtained from rock salts. It is soluble in water and quick-acting. The potash in wood ashes is also soluble in water if screened from the bonfire and stored; the ash must be kept dry. Lime may be obtained either as hydrated (slaked) lime (calcium hydroxide) or ground limestone (chalk, calcium carbonate), the latter being the form usually employed in composts.

In a well-balanced compost there should be ample plant food, sufficient in fact to bring short-lived and quick-growing plants to maturity without further recourse to fertilizers. On the other hand, with slow-growing perennial plants, for example, pot shrubs or certain bulbs which may be grown in pots for a long period, feeding by liquid fertilizers is very desirable.

The use of such liquid fertilizers for feeding can undoubtedly be overdone and they must always be applied with caution; nevertheless, used with common sense they can make a wonderful difference either to pot plants or to crops in the open. Bear in mind that while a little is without doubt beneficial, an overdose may be disastrous. The safest way for the novice who is afraid of overdosing is to use one of the advertised complete fertilizers and never to exceed the strength recommended by the manufacturer.

Special manures are prepared for chrysanthemums, carnations, vines, etc.

It is never wise for the novice to mix fertilizers, as in many cases an adverse chemical reaction is set up.

Never a year passes but we are introduced to some new product of the chemical laboratories. Sometimes a fuss is made of them for a year or so and they quietly fade away. On the other hand they may, like the rooting hormones, be of such importance that they revolutionize the technique of the particular operation for which they were introduced. At the present moment the subject of most interest is giberellic acid and its effect on the growth of plants. It is as yet only in the experimental stage, but microscopic amounts have produced fantastic increases in growth, and it may prove to be of considerable value.

3 · Greenhouse Routine

Atmospheric Moisture

One of the main reasons why many plants dislike the atmosphere of the domestic room is that it is kept too dry. The reaction to dry or humid conditions varies from plant to plant. Cacti and succulents of course will thrive under extremely dry conditions; they are naturally plants from arid semi-desert parts of the world and will rot if kept too damp in the winter. On the other hand, many foliage plants revel in humid atmospheric conditions. They are, in fact, from the opposite extreme, the steamy conditions of the tropical jungle, and cannot tolerate hot, dry air without losing most of their principal attraction, their bold and striking foliage. Hence it becomes obvious that in a small greenhouse one cannot grow everything successfully. As so often in other walks of life, one has to compromise and either specialize in one extreme or the other, or go in for the more tolerant kinds of plants which is the course adopted by most amateur gardeners.

DAMPING. A certain amount of atmospheric humidity then is necessary to counter the drying effect of artificial heating. The usual and generally most satisfactory method is to damp with a watering can the floor, paths, and walls each morning, and if possible at midday. In winter, however, it must not be done too late in the day and often may not be necessary. This moisture is absorbed by brick-work or stone-work and gradually given back to the air to create the desired degree of humidity. The amount necessary varies with the materials of which the house is built, brick being best, and then concrete; metal of course being non-absorbent.

An experienced grower can sense or feel the degree of humidity instantly, and it is one of the things one learns by experience. During spring and summer when plenty of ventilation is being used the garden syringe is a valuable ally. For some kinds of plants, ferns, for example, it is only necessary to spray or damp the atmosphere or the stagings on which the plants are growing.

Other kinds of plants will benefit from direct syringing. This also has the effect of keeping in check the pest known as red spider, which thrives on dry conditions. Though a necessary part of greenhouse routine, damping must not be overdone in cool houses, as too high a degree of humidity causes soft growth and predisposes the plant to fungus disease. On the staging screened boiler ashes are first-class for holding moisture and gradually diffusing it; small gravel, of course, looks better, but a greater depth is necessary to give the same result.

It is obvious that the moisture needed will vary from day to day with weather conditions. In wet weather little may be needed; in foggy weather none at all, for the atmosphere is already charged with moisture and to continue damping would only aggravate bad conditions. In this case a little more pipe heat and a crack of air on the top ventilators is beneficial in order to dry out the air.

The point was made earlier that no damping should be done late in the day, and this perhaps requires a little explanation. Temperatures fall somewhat at night and this causes condensation on the glass. In most up-to-date houses the glazing is designed to allow this to run off, but if it is excessive, drops will collect and fall on the plants. Being cold, they can do quite a lot of damage to flowers and foliage and still more to seed pan or seedlings. The obvious answer then is not too much moisture in the evenings or, alternatively, slightly more artificial heat to keep up the temperature, and the first is without question the economical course to follow.

WATERING. A question very frequently heard and one of the most exasperating is, 'How often should I water such and such a plant?' To be quite honest one cannot give a definite answer, as so many factors enter into it. I know from bitter experience that it is one of the most difficult operations in horticulture for the beginner. You simply cannot say give it so much water once a week. It depends entirely on the conditions at the moment, on the time of year, the kind of house, the position within the house, and perhaps even more on the compost in which it is growing and whether or not the pot is full of roots and growing vigorously. The only thing you can be definite about is that when it becomes dry, or shows signs of becoming dry, it should be thoroughly soaked, from the spout of the can and not a rose, so that all the soil in the pot becomes wet. To damp the surface, leaving the bulk of the compost dry, is one of the quickest ways of killing a plant, as, though it may look moist, the fine root hairs which feed the plant will die. The reverse course, watering too liberally, can also cause trouble; drainage becomes choked, the plant is water-logged, and again the fine root hairs may die through lack of air. Waterlogging, by the way, is easily corrected first by laying the plant on its side and draining, then by knocking it out of its pot carefully and cleaning out the crocks at the bottom of the pot.

How then is one to hit the happy medium and give the neces-sary amount of water for the health and growth of the plant? The time-honoured method is to tap the pot with a tapping mallet, simply a cane with a little wooden hammer head. If the plant is dry it will 'ring', if wet the response is a dull thud. Beware, how-ever, of the cracked pot, which will not ring and may give a false impression. As the grower becomes more experienced this may not be necessary except when in doubt. Weight is also a pretty good indication; if the pot feels light it is dry; if heavy, it is wet. Watering is simply a matter of experience, by no means difficult but varying enormously with the type of compost used, depending on whether the plant is well rooted or recently potted, and on current atmospheric conditions. The amount of leaf surface pre-sented by the plant and consequent transpiration must also be kept in mind. A plant which is really dry and 'flagging', that is to say with its leaves flaccid, should be placed in a bucket of water and left until the 'ball' is thoroughly soaked.

One other method of watering has much to recommend it, particularly in winter. This requires a shallow tray or trough with an inch or two of water. Plants which dislike water round the collar, or which tend to rot there, can be stood in this tray for the water to soak up through the ball. It is a great deal safer with many plants than surface watering. This method is also of value with seed pots, particularly where the seed sown is small and easily dislodged by using the water-pot even with a fine rose. Using the rose when watering is a frequent cause of casualties in winter through cold water lodging in the crown of the plants.

Watering Cans. For greenhouse work what is known as a Haw's pattern (1 gallon) is the most convenient. It is handled by the bar from opening to spout and is beautifully balanced. There is a good length of spout and the volume poured is not so great that it is likely to wash the compost out of the pots, which can happen with a larger type of spout.

Two roses are supplied, a coarse one for damping down and a fine one for watering seedlings, etc. Too large a can makes heavy work of watering plants on stagings, but a 2-gallon can, Haw's No. 4, is quicker for watering large pots at ground level. A very small can designed for the more inaccessible shelves is Haw's No. 1 (2 quarts).

Equally important is the type and quality of the syringe used. For a small house a dual purpose type will be sufficient. Its main purpose is forcible syringing of plants, but by means of a different type of nozzle it also serves for the application of insecticides. These are expensive, but with careful handling will give years of service. For larger houses it is worth while getting a 2-inch bore syringe also, as it is considerably quicker, and has greater volume for forcible syringing.

Liquid Feeding

The oldest method of liquid feeding, and for those who live in the country and can obtain it, the best, is fresh liquid manure diluted by about ten times its volume of water. The easy way is to plunge a small sack of manure in a barrel of water and dilute as required. Soot may be used in the same way. An alternative is to obtain an old, but serviceable, galvanized tank and partition it with perforated zinc, placing the manure or soot at one end and dipping from the other.

Plant nutrients are now made up either as dry fertilizers or in liquid form. Two made up to the John Innes formula are J.I.D. (dry) feeds, which is placed on the ball of the plants dry and watered in, the rate of application recommended being half to one teaspoonful to a 5-inch pot; and J.I.L. (liquid) feed, in which the fertilizer is used at half to one ounce in one gallon of soft water. The formula is actually the same except that a 'carrier' is added for the dry feed.

There are also a number of proprietary liquid feeds advertised with varying analyses so that the proportions are known. The essential is that they should be balanced, that is, contain all three essential nutrients: nitrogen, phosphorus, and potash in their correct proportions. Too much nitrogen tends to make plants leafy and luxuriant but soft and frequently shy of flowering. With such plants a dressing of bone meal and wood ashes would be more beneficial than a compound fertilizer.

How often to feed depends on season, environment, and condition of the plants. Recently potted plants will not need it, nor will it be wise to feed from September to March when growth and development are slowed down. About every ten days during the summer months would be safe. The cooler plants are grown, the less is feeding likely to be required. Dull weather will also slow down growth and less feeding will be necessary.

Always water a dry plant before giving either feeds or top dressing, as damage may be done to the roots otherwise. Keep in mind also that feeding should be 'little and often', and above all do not exceed the concentrations recommended by the makers.

Shelves

With many of the prefabricated houses, shelves are included either fitted from the eaves or slung in the centre under the ridge.

They can be extremely useful, but one has to bear in mind that they also cast shadows and to some extent reduce the amount of light obtained by the plants on the benches. Their greatest advantage lies in getting plants up close to the glass, particularly in winter, and keeping them sturdy and dwarf.

Shelves can in fact be employed throughout the year for one purpose or another. In winter they can be used for such bulbous plants as lachenalia and freesia. Once these are in bud the shelves are excellent for seedlings such as early vegetable crops; for example, onions and brassicas, and as these are large enough to be 'hardened off', their place can be taken by flowering 'annuals' such as antirrhinums, tagetes, lobelia. By the time these are 'hardened off' the sun is gaining power and the shelf can then be used to ripen off the freesias, lachenalias, nerines, and similar bulbs and corms which have finished flowering and for which thorough maturing is essential.

Ventilation and Temperature Control

Plants must have plenty of fresh air, it is as vital to them as to ourselves. Without some circulation of air, plants will never be sturdy and strong. This does not of course mean that ventilators can be thrown wide open in winter; obviously they to a great extent control temperature, and to maintain an even temperature they have to be used with discretion.

In many modern greenhouses they are under the control of thermostats, as previously noted. It does not by any means follow that the more pipe-heat plants are given the better they will be, too much often has the effect of making them drawn and weak.

It is often better, particularly from October to March when light conditions are poor, to keep temperatures as low as safety permits, admitting as much air as is possible without subjecting the plants to cold draughts. Cold cutting winds can be devastating and it is always bad policy to open ventilators on the windward side. Large houses should have side ventilators in addition to those on the ridge and the older types had also what are called 'box' ventilators (Plate 22). These are fitted so that air is admitted almost directly on to the hot-water pipes where it is warmed. The rising air causes a circulation without appreciably lowering the temperature.

22. Box ventilators and top ventilation.

A point to watch in summer is that early morning sunshine can cause a rapid rise in temperature under glass, so ventilation should be given early on sunny mornings. It is also advisable, in order to conserve as much sun heat as possible, to close the house immediately the sun is off it, and the temperature falls.

Ventilation must always be considered according to prevailing weather conditions, not done by the clock. Some form of shading is necessary in summer to prevent scorching, and to keep down excessively high temperatures. The most satisfactory method is by means of blinds.

They may be of the roller type in which cotton or similar material is unrolled from the ridge over the slope of the greenhouse or what are called lath blinds (Plate 23). These work on the same principle but, being much heavier, are made in shorter lengths which are pulled up and down by ropes from the bottom.

23. Lath blinds on a mixed plant house.

The alternative method is to colour-wash the exterior of the glass from about April to September with either a green or white stipple. The best and most permanent type contains size and is washed on while warm. It will usually remain on until September, when it has to be removed to maintain the best possible conditions of light. The disadvantage of this or any other stippling materials is that it keeps the house too dark in dull sunless weather.

With blinds, only the sunny side of the house need be shaded. In September the blinds may be taken off, dried, and stored in a dry place until March or April.

Shading can be quite a problem with a mixed collection, e.g. Australian plants, carnations, and cacti never require it, whereas soft-foliage plants would be scorched without it. The best compromise is to move all plants that do not want shade outside for the summer.

Arrangement

One of the most common errors in gardening, and especially under glass, is overcrowding. Having raised them one is always loath to discard seedlings or rooted cuttings which are really surplus. Though well aware of the necessity, I still find it difficult to discard a good plant. To do plants justice each one must be given sufficient light and air. If this is not given they must compete for both, and as a result they become 'drawn' and spindly instead of sturdy well-balanced plants.

Another all too common mistake is to try and crowd in too diverse a range of material. Some kinds of plant never mix well; they require different cultural conditions which make it almost impossible to grow all well, the only possible way being to segregate them in groups so that those requiring humidity, fuchsias, for example, may be given a cool shady corner where they can be freely damped and syringed, while those requiring drier conditions, e.g. pelargoniums, should be given the lightest, most airy situation and kept on the dry side. The overplanting of climbing plants also, particularly strong growers, may cause too much shade and do harm to the plants on the benches. These should be thinned out in the autumn or after flowering in any case, to admit as much light as possible during autumn and winter.

The staging of the plants may be done either in a decorative manner or in rows, depending on whether the material is foliage and flowering plants for display, or plants being grown on to maturity, e.g. tomato plants.

If it is display material no pains should be spared in placing and arranging them to best advantage. It is often necessary to raise plants by placing them on a half brick or inverted pot to get the best effect, and if this is done something bushy or fairly dense should be placed in front to hide the brick or pot. Plants grown for their foliage only, such as grevillea, eucalyptus, or grasses like the variegated *Miscanthus*, are particularly useful in breaking a flat effect.

Plants of pendulous habit which will drape the front of the stage are useful for breaking up the hard line of the edge of the staging; three useful plants for the purpose are the variegated-leaved *Zebrina pendula* (the wandering Jew), the closely allied *Tradescantia* with green and white foliage *T. fluminensis* variety, or the small-leaved forms of *Coleus blumei* such as *C. whittonii*. The greenhouse campanula *C. isophylla* and its varieties are also excellent for this purpose. Between these pendulous plants small edging plants such as African violets and *Pilea* are good.

Natural Layout. For reasons of economy many growers are arranging their benches as small naturally planted gardens. There is no doubt that plants thrive in this way, the root run is more free and natural, growth is usually quicker, and watering is cut down to the absolute minimum. Disadvantages are that plants are less mobile than when in pots, they are not so easy for flower show purposes, nor can they be taken into the house readily. Another point is that one certainly cannot grow so many different kinds in the same area. Nevertheless by artistic grouping and layout this method can be very satisfying and it does cut down maintenance tremendously.

Some excellent examples of this treatment may be seen at Kew in the Sherman Hoyt house and small South African house. The latter is particularly worthy of notice, as different kinds of stone are cleverly worked in for different succulent plants. This method of cultivation is well adapted to low-growing and creeping types of plant. Ferns I have mentioned, and selaginellas are equally good. All kinds of succulents and cacti may be so used and the tall columnar types of cacti give excellent contrast in form with the sprawling habits of others and the compact rosettes of the *Aeonium* and *Echeveria* group. Many kinds of foliage plants can also be used, and groups of small plants, such as saintpaulia, amongst them, can give both colour and interest. The same method is also suitable for many tender 'bulbous' plants which give a wonderful display in season, though there is the disadvantage that while bulbs are dormant the site is naked and uninteresting. It is not easy to interplant as the bulbs require hot, dry conditions for ripening.

Before starting bear in mind that the additional weight involved may well be in hundredweights, or, if the area is large, tons, so do not attempt it until you are certain that your benches are strong enough to carry such a burden. Concrete benches carried on pre-cast supports or on brick piers are safe, but light benches of asbestos or corrugated iron with light metal legs are not built for this weight and are definitely unsafe.

The essentials are stone of good appearance, preferably a quantity of the same kind, and if it is rugged and weather-worn so much the better. By this I do not mean the water-worn limestone so widely used for rock gardens. Sandstone is generally more useful for this purpose as it holds moisture so much better.

If you are using a centre stage some degree of height is desirable and some of the larger pieces should be kept for the purpose.

Most benches are fitted with an upturned rim and have drainage holes, or, in the case of the prefabricated sections, cracks between the sections, which ensure free drainage. If this is not so, it is essential to drill a few holes in the bench. Next, level up to the rim with coarse material. For succulents and cacti this could be broken brick or pots put through a crock-breaking machine, but for ferns or bromeliads a thick layer of dead bracken rhizomes, or fibre of this type, would be more suitable. For the majority of other plants one needs a good layer of drainage material with leaves or similar roughage over the holes to prevent the soil choking the outlets. All that remains is to lay the stone and fill up with a good compost such as J.I. Potting Compost.

The next step is to build round the perimeter, using stone not more than 2 to 4 inches thick and if possible letting it overlap the edge slightly to give a more natural line. Some irregularity in size, shape, and thickness of stone used is desirable to break the formal rectangle. It is worth while anchoring these in place with a dab of cement to prevent them being easily knocked out of place later.

Subsequent building must depend on area and plants to be used; the effect desired is much the same as that used by nursery-men in the 'table' gardens shown at Chelsea and Vincent Square with Alpines in particular. With a bench only a few feet square no attempt should be made to build up, but the larger stones may be used as island sites for the most suitable specimens and the remaining stone used to arrange suitable planting bays. For side benches small stones are preferable; in any case, a shallow arrangement is suitable.

Where the centre stage of an old house is in poor or dangerous condition it may be worth while to scrap it and to plant it out as a permanent border. It is worth while raising it a couple of feet above path level preferably by a stone wall. The use of the same type of stone to break up the level of the surface also looks well. For such a centre a good range of tender flowering shrubs, foliage plants, and ferns could be used. An excellent example of this kind of planting is the centre of the temperate house at Wisley which always has something of interest to show.

Hygiene

Greenhouse hygiene is extremely important, and clean, healthy plants are unlikely unless it is kept constantly in mind. The term covers the immediate removal of diseased material, dead leaves, and rubbish of all kinds, control and eradication of weeds and insect pests, and the annual scrubbing down of both glass and structure.

Bad winter weather affords the opportunity to give the green-house its annual clean-up. Glass and woodwork should be scrubbed down with soft soap and water or a weak solution of

C

carbolic or similar disinfectant. If the house can be emptied for a few days the commercial practice of spraying with a 1 per cent solution of cresylic acid in water is quicker than scrubbing. If stages are of timber, these should also be thoroughly scrubbed. For solid benches the material used on the stage should be renewed, or if shingle, washed. Painting or minor repairs can also be dealt with at this time, or it may be more convenient to do this in summer when the house can be more easily emptied. The clean-up should also include the washing of pots and pans, sterilization of seed boxes, stakes, and canes.

Weed control both inside the house and nearby is more important than is at first apparent. Weeds are very often hosts for pests and diseases, and if they are allowed to breed and multiply on the doorstep it will not be long before pests are also present in the house. Aphis, for example, flourish on a number of weeds, and so do white fly and red spider during hot, dry weather. Weeds should therefore be kept down. Their place is on the compost heap, together with thinnings and prunings, and other rubbish from the greenhouse.

For glass-washing, whether it be the scrubbing down, removal of stippling in autumn, or the cleaning off of soot and dirt in winter, a most useful aid is a car-cleaning outfit. This is simply a long hollow handle linked with a hosepipe, the water passing up the handle and through the attached mop head on to the glass.

Plant Propagation

The art of propagating or increasing plants in number is to most people the most interesting and diverse of any aspect of gardening.

It requires study and experience to become really proficient, as there are so many different types of plant and alternative methods used even for the same plant. Nevertheless, nature's own method is usually by seeds, and wherever possible this is undoubtedly the best. There are, however, many cases where seeds cannot be obtained, or if obtained would not breed true to the parent stock, and then what we term vegetative propagation must be adopted in one form or another.

PLANTS FROM SEEDS. Success in raising plants from seeds will depend to a considerable extent on the provision of suitable conditions, the most important being temperature, moisture, and compost.

Without question seeds are the cheapest way of raising a stock, where it can be used. It is surprising what a number of seedlings, of annuals for example, may be raised from a packet costing no more than a shilling or so. I would, however, emphasize that it pays to give a little more for a selected strain and that, conversely, it is folly to buy the cheapest. This takes up the same amount of space, the same time and labour, and you have an inferior plant to show for it at the end.

Like most things in horticulture, seeds vary in their requirements and one cannot be dogmatic. Speaking generally, however, a temperature of about 60° F. is sufficient for all temperate plants and should cover most of those referred to in this book.

Some seeds germinate better in the dark, while others are known to do better in light. In practice most of them will germinate if protected only from bright sunshine.

The great majority of seeds require no preparation before sowing, but there are a few, such for example as *Canna*, which are as hard as a bullet. There are several methods of speeding up the softening of these seed coats. The most generally practised is, as with sweet peas, filing or nicking the seed coat to allow the penetration of water. Legumes (e.g. *Acacia*) which are too small to handle easily may be soaked in boiling water or even placed on a shovel and heated for a moment over a fire to break the bone-hard seed coat; another method is to place them on a sheet of newspaper and burn this, then sow immediately. An alternative method is to place the seeds in a saucer and rub with the base of a flower pot, scoring the surface of the seeds.

The preparation of different composts for a range of plants is generally unnecessary, a light, well-drained compost being suitable for most (see Chapter 2). The notable exception is the peat-loving group in which the soil must be free of lime and preferably chiefly of peat and sand. Certain kinds of alpine plants also do better with a greater proportion of sand to increase the drainage, and at the other extreme for water-loving plants a little

24. Preparation of the seed box, using roughage to improve the drainage.

25. Firming the compost with the fingers.

26. Firming and levelling the soil to obtain an even surface.

27. Watering the boxes before sowing. Note that sufficient depth has been left for effective watering.

chopped sphagnum moss may be added to retain an even degree of moisture.

The development of the J.I. seed compost has simplified the procedure so far as the great majority of plants are concerned. If this is not readily obtainable, mix your own as near to the formula as you can. Keep in mind that it must be open and well drained and must not be used either too wet or too dry. Drainage is important and so is the use of clean pots. When preparing the receptacles the soil should be made firm but not rammed hard or the tiny roots will find it difficult to penetrate. A circular wooden presser is usually used, but the bottom of a pot of the same size as that used for sowing will do the job of firming and levelling. Don't fill to the top of the pot or it will be impossible to water properly later. At least a quarter of an inch should be left, even with small sizes. The soil should be well watered first and then left to drain off for an hour or so when it will be ready for sowing.

28. Sowing, spacing out the seed (where large enough) with the fingers.

29. Sifting a fine layer of compost over the seeds. Here the label has been inserted, but if glass has to be used it is usually laid horizontally or tacked to the end of the box.

A small frame of some kind is most useful. Even a soap box covered with glass sheets will serve, but most economic in the long run is probably one of the rustless metal frames now available in several sizes. They will keep the atmosphere humid and avoid the necessity for too frequent watering of the seed pots. A case or frame of this kind also makes it unnecessary to cover each individual pot with glass, though this is still desirable with very fine seed such as *Streptocarpus* and *Begonia*. Another advantage is that in really sunny weather a sheet of paper or similar material can be placed over the whole frame – a much easier and quicker job than covering individual pots and pans. The frames should be checked daily and pots showing signs of germination should be brought out into the light and given drier conditions, or they will rapidly become 'drawn' and weak.

Probably the most frequent mistake in sowing is to sow too thickly. When germination takes place there is a struggle for existence, the seedlings become drawn, and unless they are pricked off immediately they will probably 'damp off'. This is a fungus disease which flourishes on just such conditions; once it starts to spread, it is extremely difficult to control. The best method of prevention is by watering the seed pots, before sowing, with Cheshunt compound (which can be obtained ready-made) or permanganate of potash at one teaspoonful to the gallon of water. The first essential is then, sow thinly, and give the seedlings maximum light and air at the earliest possible moment. In sowing fine seed, it is an old dodge to mix it thoroughly with dry sand, when it will spread much more evenly over the surface.

Another frequent cause of failure is to cover the seed too thickly. This is a point which only experience can teach, but the old gardener's rule of covering only to the depth of the seed itself has a lot of common sense in it. In effect it means that dust-like seeds, such as *Begonia*, *Streptocarpus* or *Lobelia*, should not be covered at all, a sheet of glass resting on the rim of the pots is all that is necessary. With larger seeds a very light sprinkling of sand or light sandy soil is usually given.

Germination depends not only on the species or variety but also on the age of the seed itself. The life of seeds, called their period of viability, varies from plant to plant. It may only be a year or

30. Covering with a sheet of glass and newspaper.

31. In this instance the seed box and pan have been covered with polythene after sowing, to prevent evaporation from the surface of the soil.

so, or it may be fifty years, but the conditions under which they are stored are important.

Home-saved seeds or surplus seeds of any kind should be kept in a cool, relatively dry, and preferably dark place. They should first be cleaned (that is to say, get rid of seed pods, old parts of the flowers, etc.), put into envelopes, and labelled correctly. A biscuit tin or similar receptacle is probably as good a method of storage as any, provided it is in a cool place. Generally speaking, the earlier they can be sown after collecting, the quicker is the germination, though there are exceptions to this. In any case the best time for sowing is obviously spring, with the whole growing season ahead.

In many plants germination can be expected in a week or two, in some a matter of days, but there are many plants whose seedlings will not be seen for a year or even longer. This point is important, for a great deal of valuable seed has been thrown away through ignorance or perhaps just impatience. There have been many instances of seed thrown away as useless germinating freely on the rubbish heap. The subsequent treatment of seedlings will vary with the type of plant; quickly maturing plants such as annuals are usually grown on in boxes until they can be planted out, slower growing plants such as tender shrubs and also plants like the brooms or acacias which resent disturbance of the roots are best pricked off singly into 72-size (2-inch) pots.

With most seedlings, once seed has germinated the earlier it is pricked off the better. If the seedlings can be transferred before fine roots are developed they will obviously be less damaged than would large seedlings with a fragile root system which, however carefully handled, must be broken and damaged in the process.

Here again there are exceptions. With many of the bulbous species and varieties such as *Lilium* and *Hippeastrum* (the amaryllis of most gardeners) I prefer to sow thinly and leave the seedlings in the seed pot without disturbance for the first year. I believe that the check in handling cancels out the advantage of pricking out. They will die down in autumn and rest until February or March. This is the time to knock them out of their pots or boxes and give them a new and richer compost and room to develop for a further year. Slow-growing species are best in pans or pots.

The latest refinement in raising plants from seed is to purchase cartons of vermiculite with fertilizer added and the seeds ready sown. They are even packed in transparent plastic containers if desired, so that they may be germinated in these and gradually given air as they germinate. All the purchaser has to do is to provide the initial watering, place in a warm situation, and see they do not dry out afterwards. Both flowers and vegetables are available.

VEGETATIVE PROPAGATION. Amongst the several methods of vegetative propagation, that of increase by cuttings is the most important and extensively practised. There is a wide variation in the best types of cuttings to use and the season at which they are best inserted. So far as the cool greenhouse is concerned, it will be mainly a question of perpetuating the collection of tender perennial plants, but I would emphasize that given greenhouse facilities a great deal wider range of material can be handled.

For rooting cuttings a closed propagating frame or case is essential (Plate 32). There are many different types of case made

32. An excellent type of timber house and propagating case; note the electric heater below the frame.

for the purpose, and a rustless metal frame (Plate 10) is probably the most economical as these are almost everlasting and relatively trouble-free. They are particularly valuable in old greenhouses where mice, woodlice, crickets, or similar visitors are troublesome. The fundamental reason for the case, however, is that cuttings, having no roots to sustain them, must be kept in a humid atmosphere to check loss of moisture.

If what is called bottom heat can be arranged, rooting will be both quicker and more certain. This can be done in various ways. If the case can be placed directly over the pipes and part of the pipes cased in under it, a steady and regular warmth is provided. The modern method of electrical soil heating by wires is now being used widely for the purpose and specially built propagating frames incorporate this method.

A propagation case will enable its owner to experiment with the rooting of all kinds of material apart from his greenhouse plants. Perennials such as lupins and delphiniums may be rooted from basal shoots produced early in spring in much the same way as with dahlias and chrysanthemums.

In summer a wide assortment of trees and shrubs, such as forsythia, lilac, and hydrangea, may be quickly propagated from soft cuttings and, later in the season, such bedding plants as violas and penstemons also. Most propagators will agree that this is the most fascinating part of horticulture.

Where no bottom heat is available such a case can still be used to advantage, but rooting will of necessity be slower, and so far as tender subjects are concerned it will not be wise to start so early in the year.

The rooting medium is of course vital. For many plants sharp sand is sufficient, but for the great majority a 2 to 1 mixture of neutral peat (of the same type as is used in the potting composts) and sand is still as good as any. In forty years' experience I have seen many different materials recommended and tried, but I have yet to find anything more generally useful. Some propagators swear by crushed pumice, some advocate finely broken crock, while the material most favoured today seems to be a selected form of vermiculite.

The essentials are free aeration and drainage coupled with ample moisture. Coarse sand alone will provide this, but the addition of peat gives the young roots something to root into immediately they are produced. If sand is used alone, the cuttings must be potted at the earliest possible moment after rooting, as there is obviously nothing for them to feed on in the sand.

TYPE OF CUTTING. An experienced propagator can tell at a glance whether a given material will or will not root. It is very largely a question of the maturity of the cutting. If taken too soft and young, many kinds will just rot, and if too hard they will take a long time to root. If one can hit the happy medium, rooting should with most kinds of plants be quick and easy. On the other hand, I have known plants, particularly evergreens and conifers, take over a year to root.

With the great majority of plants, cuttings for indoor propagation are made some 2 to 4 inches long, the lower leaves are trimmed off, and the cut is made immediately below a joint or node. This is because any stem left below a joint would in most

74

cases decay, and once this starts the rot could easily go right through the cutting.

Cuttings are of two types, hardwood, mostly trees and shrubs, and softwood, for example, herbaceous perennials such as *Coleus* and begonias.

Two methods of inserting cuttings are employed. Where a large quantity of a kind is required a bed is prepared in the case and the cuttings are lined out, either with a blunt-pointed stick known as a 'dibber', or into a slit cut into the bed with a knife or similar implement. On the other hand, if a small number each of several or many kinds are being inserted, it is more convenient to put them round the rim of 3-inch pots and sink these in the bed of the case. The advantages are, firstly, that the pot serves to provide extra aeration, and it is often found that difficult plants will do better this way, and, secondly, the quicker rooting subjects can be taken out and the vacant space used again, without disturbing the rest of the cuttings. There are certain kinds of plant which make only one or two rather brittle roots, for example, acacias and some ceanothus, and with these it is as well to root each cutting separately in very small pots to avoid having to transfer them while small.

When inserting it is important to make sure that the base of the cutting is touching the bottom of the hole you have made, and that they are as firm as the cutting medium allows. At the same time it is a good practice to place a layer of sand on the surface of the bed or pot so that when the cutting is inserted a little sand falls into the hole and surrounds the base of the cutting. With soft cuttings the depth of insertion should be one-quarter to one-third the length of the cutting, but with harder wood it may be more. Deeper insertion does not help rooting, rather the reverse, as it increases the risk of loss by rotting.

The distance apart of the cuttings will in both cases depend on their size. With most they should almost but not quite touch, but in dealing with tough and leathery-leaved plants such as ericas, they can be closely packed and take no harm.

After insertion they should be thoroughly watered and kept closely shut down, except for a daily airing, until signs of growth indicate that rooting is taking place. During hot weather both shading and syringing may be necessary. More air may then be admitted and the cuttings gradually hardened off. After a week or two in the cutting pots they can be potted off separately into 60-size pots. They are usually given a few days in the case after potting to re-establish and settle down, and then again hardened off gradually, by giving more light and air. During the time the cuttings are in the case a moderate degree of humidity must be maintained. A temperature of 60°F. to 70°F. will suit most temperate plants. They must be looked over daily and the water condensed on the glass should be wiped off with a cloth. If this is not done it will form drops and fall on to the cuttings, often causing them to rot. For the same reason all dead or decaying leaves should be removed immediately.

Spring and summer are the best seasons for propagating most indoor plants. Tender bedding plants such as perennial calceolarias, pelargoniums (geraniums), and penstemons are usually rooted in autumn in shallow boxes and carried through the winter in frost-free frames or in the greenhouse. In certain cases it is better to pot up a stock plant or two and carry these under glass ready to propagate in spring. Examples are named varieties of heliotrope, and double lobelia.

It is generally true that cuttings from young shoots are easier to root, and it is an old gardener's practice to cut woody plants hard back after flowering to make them produce new shoots for cuttings.

ROOT-FORMING SUBSTANCES. There are now a number of synthetic root-forming preparations on the market which will speed up rooting. Different strengths are prepared for hard and soft cuttings, and provided the makers' instructions are followed they can be relied on to give quicker results. Where only a limited number of cuttings are being handled the powdered material in which the growth substance is mixed with talc powder is the most convenient. These preparations are no substitute for skill and experience and it must not be thought that they will root anything and everything.

LEAF CUTTINGS. Another distinctive kind of propagation which is used for only a limited number of plants makes use of the leaves. The best known is the begonia, particularly the lovely *B. rex* varieties. The leaves are cut and laid either on the bed of the propagating frame, or preferably in pans. The main veins of the leaf are severed in several places and the leaf pinned down or anchored by a stone. In a very short time small plants form above the cuts. These soon develop roots and can be potted up as new plants. Similar are saintpaulia (African violet) leaves. These are cut with an inch or so of stalk attached, which is inserted to the base of the leaf blade in sand. In a very short time a young plant develops at the base of the leaf. Gloxinias also may be raised in this way, usually when the leaves are fully developed. The only difference is that in this case a small tuber is produced which is kept dormant until spring. If it is desired to propagate numbers of a particularly good variety, the leaves may be treated like begonias and the veins severed, when small tubers will be produced. Some of the named varieties of *Streptocarpus* are also propagated by leaf cuttings. The old leaf usually dies, leaving a young plant in its place.

Another ancient method of propagation has recently been modernized and is now extensively used. This is what used to be called marcottage, or air-layering. It is used for rooting the tops or branches of plants which have become tall or leggy. A ring is cut round the stem or a constriction made with wire. A ball of moss is then tied over the wounded area and kept moist. The up-to-date procedure is to envelop the moss in a plastic cover to keep it evenly moist until rooted. Under glass it is used for cordylines and dracaenas and such plants as the variegated manihot – in fact anything which does not root readily as cuttings.

The method of taking leaf-bud cuttings is also an old one, but has recently come into prominence in connexion with the propagation of camellias (Plate 33). It differs from the leaf cuttings of saintpaulia or begonia in that a growth bud is present in the leaf axil when inserted, and it is the bud and not the leaf which produces the new plant. The cutting is made in autumn an inch or so long, the stem being cut in two, and half of it inserted with the leaf and bud. Roots are developed from the cut surface, and the

33. The different types of cutting which may be used for camellia. The two top rows are internodal cuttings, the third heel cuttings, and the lower are leaf-bud cuttings.

bud commences to grow. 'Leaf-bud' cuttings are also used for arbutus, holly, rhododendrons, etc.

What are termed 'eyes' are a similar kind of propagation. This is used with vines in particular and similar plants. In this case the cutting is again an inch or so long and split into two. The half with the bud is pressed horizontally, bud uppermost, on to the propagating material, and will eventually root with the bud starting to grow. The difference is that being a deciduous plant no leaf is present. These dormant buds are inserted about January in a warm case, usually each in a small pot.

Some of the lily family will produce small bulbs at the base of the leaves, if these are treated as leaf cuttings, the best known example being *Lachenalia*. The leaves are inserted in a sandy compost in much the same way as ordinary leaf cuttings. One of the best ways of increasing true lilies (i.e. *Lilium* species and varieties) is by detaching scales from the bulbs and treating them in much the same way as a cutting (Plate 34). They are half buried in a light sandy compost or in pure sand, and placed in a shaded situation. Small plants are produced in a month or so at the base of the scale and these are either potted separately or, if there are a number, put into pans (Plate 35). For this purpose pots or pans are better than boxes, as they can be left alone for a year or so to build up and boxes tend to go to pieces.

Many of the natural methods of reproduction also help to increase stock and still keep it true to type. Offsets from the bulbs of tulips, narcissus and many others, bulbils produced naturally in the leaf axils of many lilies, and what are called spawn on the corms of many of the iris family, such as freesias and gladiolus, all afford an easy means of increase.

DIVISION. Probably the best example of this method is amongst ferns. These are not so easy to raise from spores, some in fact never produce them. In any case many of the crested forms do not reproduce true to type. The most reliable way, then, is to divide the plant early in the year. If left until growth is active the plant is badly shaken up and takes quite a while to recover, but if done while still inactive, in most ferns about February, the new plants soon recover and make new growth. Many of the tuberous-rooted herbaceous plants, such as *Canna* and *Hedychium*, also increase freely by means of division of the roots while dormant. The plants are simply knocked out of their old pots and the youngest and most vigorous pieces replanted, the rest being discarded. They are potted into new compost and given a warmer, closer atmosphere until growing freely. Careful watering is essential until the roots are developed.

Other plants in which this method is used are foliage plants, particularly those with variegated leaves which would not come true from seed. Examples are the variegated varieties of *Liriope*

34. Scale propagation of lilies, showing young plants six months after insertion of the scales.

muscari, Ophiopogon jaburan, and an old friend *Aspidistra lurida*. The variegated grasses, such as *Miscanthus sinensis* varieties, and the striking *Arundo donax variegata*, can also be treated in this way.

Propagation by root cuttings, though freely used with hardy herbaceous plants, is not extensively done under glass. Plants

35. Scale propagation, the same bulbs as in Plate 34 two years after propagation.

which can be increased in this way are *Bouvardia* and *Clerodendrums* such as *C. speciosissimum (fallax)* and *C. fragrans*. The sundews, *Drosera* species, are also usually propagated in this way, and another example is *Plumbago rosea*. The roots are cut into lengths from 1 to 1½ inches long and inserted vertically in pots so that the tops of the cuttings are level with the top of the soil. A compost of equal parts loam, peat, and sand is used. They must be placed in the propagating case with a minimum temperature of 60° F. and will begin to grow in two or three weeks.

As a general rule the amateur does not attempt either grafting or budding and it is an open question whether the subject should be discussed in a book of this kind. By this I do not imply that it is too difficult, but that the amateur gardener simply does not have to hand the assortment of stocks on which to bud or graft, nor does he generally have the nursery space in which to grow them. This is not so extensively practised under greenhouse work as in fruit growing and general nursery work. Both subjects are fully discussed in The Royal Horticultural Society's *Dictionary of Gardening* and various methods of grafting well illustrated.

36. Slow-rooting cuttings are sometimes enclosed in polythene bags. This shows the method used at Wisley.

PROPAGATION UNDER POLYTHENE. This material, though admitting light and allowing gases to escape through it, does not allow water to pass. It is in consequence now being utilized by the plant propagator in various ways of which air-layering is perhaps best known. The latest development is that of sealing cuttings in polythene bags and constructing tents of this material over cuttings inserted in the usual way (Plate 36), and also over pots and pans of seedlings (Plate 31). So far as cuttings are concerned results are said to be excellent, but with seed there is the complication that the humid atmosphere in the container is equally congenial for fungi, moulds, and algae; it will require thorough sterilization of materials and great care to avoid these evils.

4 · Shrubs for the Cool Greenhouse

Tender shrubs may be said to be the backbone of any collection of plants. First, a word of warning. There are two temptations facing the greenhouse owner, both equally difficult to resist. Overstocking is perhaps the worse; it is so easy to build up stocks during the summer and so difficult to find the accommodation for everything in winter. The second is to try and grow plants which require a higher winter minimum temperature than you are able to provide. There is, however, such an extensive range of near-hardy material available that there is really no excuse for this.

Many of the plants mentioned here, especially amongst the more woody ones, only need a little protection during the winter months, leaving the house free during the summer for a crop of tomatoes, cucumbers, etc. For this purpose it would be wise to select those which flower in autumn, winter, and early spring, even to the extent of using gently forced hardy shrubs.

To avoid damage by wind and weather and also to check too rapid drying out in hot weather, the usual practice is to plunge the pots to the rims in beds of sharp weathered ashes or sand, in an open, sunny situation. Treated in this way they are healthier and cleaner and certainly more free of insect pests than when kept permanently under glass. It also ensures well-ripened growth at least in a reasonably sunny year. They must not, however, be neglected; they must be watered freely when necessary and regularly fed with liquid fertilizers to build up their flowering buds. The following selection may all be grown with a winter minimum temperature of 45°F.:

Brunfelsia calycina macrantha is one of the most free-flowering of greenhouse shrubs and quite easy to grow. It has large violet-blue flowers produced from spring onwards. An excellent pot shrub, it may be grown on for a number of years.

Calceolaria. The shrubby types of this genus are a good deal easier to grow than are the herbaceous strains raised from seed. They are hybrids in which *C. integrifolia* and *C. rugosa*, both sub-shrubs, have played a part. The best known are *C. clibrani* and *C. banksii*, which are perpetuated by means of cuttings in late summer in much the same way as the bedding varieties. Plants flowered in 5-inch pots may be pruned back after flowering and grown on for 7-inch specimen plants for the following spring. Those already in large pots should be cut back moderately hard and the new side shoots produced taken as cuttings. During summer and early autumn these will root readily in a closed cold frame.

Cytisus canariensis is the 'Genista' of the florist, a valuable spring-flowering shrub with yellow flowers sweetly scented. It may be gently forced for Easter, should be lightly pruned after flowering, and stood out of doors. It should never be allowed to become dry once the buds are formed.

Datura. Though most striking in flower, these tender woody species do require a good deal of room. *D. suaveolens*, the 'Angel's Trumpet', has huge white trumpet-shaped flowers, and *D. sanguinea* similar flowers, but orange-red in colour. *D. cornigera* is also white, and best known by its double form *D. knightii* (Plate 37). They are almost hardy and at one time were grown in huge tubs and wintered dry in sheds and orangeries.

Diplacus. Summer flowering. *D. glutinosus* is a small greenhouse shrub from North-west America which is a useful pot plant for the greenhouse. There is a range of colour from *aurantiacus*, orange-yellow, to *puniceus*, deep maroon. They are easily propagated by means of cuttings in late summer.

Fuchsias. Not only are these among the most effective of greenhouse plants but they are also particularly suitable for sunny windows, etc., in the house. They are among the easiest of plants to propagate by means of cuttings, rooting at any time other than mid-winter. In a propagating case soft young cuttings can be rooted from February onwards, but without this March or April is early enough. Many growers prefer August-rooted plants, but these do require both room and attention during the winter months and I question if much is gained. There are many different ways in which they can be trained. The most natural is bush form in which the tips are taken out or 'stopped' twice and then allowed to grow naturally.

37. Daturas are best grown on single stems to a height of 4 or 5 feet in order to show the striking pendulous flowers to advantage.

38. A well-furnished standard fuchsia standing out of doors for the summer.

To form standards the cutting is grown on without stopping, but side growths are rubbed out until the required height is reached, usually about 4 feet (Plate 38). Another form once very popular is the pyramid. To form these the young plants are stopped once to make them break. A leader is then selected and tied to a strong cane and three or four laterals left. When these have reached 6 or 8 inches they are stopped and after an interval the leader is stopped and the whole process repeated until the desired height is reached.

The genus is hardier than is generally supposed, and to save space in winter the pots can be plunged in ashes in cold frames.

39. Fuchsia 'Falling Star', one of many up-to-date varieties.

The method we have practised for many years is first to dry the plants off so that the foliage is discarded, then plunge in a frame deep enough to take most of the growth. When this is done fill in between the branches with dry leaves right to the top of the frame. Plunged in this way they do not dry out too drastically. They can be unpacked in spring, lightly pruned and started into growth, repotting when some new growth has been made. Taller plants and standards will, of course, have to be kept in the greenhouse, or other frost-free structure. There is a thriving Fuchsia Society who publish an annual, while competitive exhibits and groups are staged every year at Vincent Square. There is a tremendous number of varieties, and choice is largely a matter of individual taste. One enterprising firm lists 400 varieties.

Hydrangeas are first-class subjects for the cool house. The correct name of the common hydrangea is now *H. macrophylla*, but it has been called *H. opuloides* and *H. hortensia*. The cultivation of well-grown plants requires both time and patience, for it is not until its second year that a well-balanced flowering plant is obtained.

Propagation is easy by cuttings. They are usually taken from April onwards, using non-flowering young shoots, three in a 60-pot, given a little bottom heat in a propagating case. When rooted they are potted singly and plunged in ashes, preferably in a cold frame. After a few days kept close and humid, they can be gradually hardened off. In July they should be stopped; that is to say, the leading shoot should be taken out and they should be moved into 5-inch pots as soon as new shoots break. They can be left in the cold frame until February, but protection must be given from frost, either by 'matting' during frost or by covering the now bare shoots with dry peat or dry leaves. From February they can be brought into the house and syringed freely to encourage growth. When growing freely regular feeding with a liquid fertilizer is desirable.

The lovely blue shades can only be obtained when the compost is on the acid side, so lime should not be used in the compost. Neither should hard water be used for watering. The 'blue' is obtained in nursery-grown stock by adding aluminium sulphate to the compost. If hard water must be used and a yellowing of the foliage results it is thought to be iron deficiency, due to the action of the lime. The up-to-date remedy is the use of sequestrol iron compounds applied as directed by the makers. Good varieties are 'Parsifal' red, 'Le Cygne' white, 'Altona' pink. For 'blueing' use 'Maréchal Foch', 'La Marné', and 'Deutschland', or 'Vicomtesse de Vibraye' (Plate 40).

Jacobinia pauciflora is one of the most reliable of near-hardy shrubs. It is compact and neat in habit, some 2 feet in height, and bears in autumn and early winter pendulous tubular flowers which are scarlet with yellow tips. The plant is sensitive

40. *Hydrangea macrophylla* 'Vicomtesse de Vibraye', a popular variety, rose-pink in most gardens, but a good blue on acid soils or when treated.

to fog and is better avoided in industrial areas where fumes and fog are prevalent. After flowering cut back a stock plant and from this obtain young cuttings in spring.

Lantanas are evergreen shrubs which can either be raised from seed or propagated vegetatively by cuttings. Named varieties should be propagated in August when cuttings will root readily in a closed case. I prefer raising from cuttings, and still think that some of the very old varieties, such as 'Chelsoni' red, 'Cloth of Gold' yellow, and 'Delicatissima' violet, are to be preferred to mixed seedlings. Old plants are cut back hard in February and given a warm situation and moister conditions, until they resume growth, when they can be repotted. Once they are established and growing freely they can be given a cooler position, a minimum of 45°F. being sufficient, and free ventilation. If necessary pinch out straggling growths to maintain a compact rounded habit.

Nerium oleander. It was once a general practice to grow these in huge tubs or pots, flower them out of doors in summer, and winter them in 'orangeries' or dry, protected shelters or sheds. They can easily be grown in pots and are delightful summer-flowering evergreen shrubs. The type is pink-flowered, but there are many shades as well as cream and white varieties and double forms. To keep them within reasonable bounds, they can be pruned back after flowering in late summer and kept on the dry side. While dry a minimum of 45°F. is quite safe. They can be repotted and started into growth in spring. They can be propagated by cuttings which root readily in late summer or early autumn.

Salvia. The shrubby species of *Salvia* are valuable plants for late summer and autumn flowering. The best known is the scarlet flowering *S. grahami* which will carry on flowering under glass long after the outdoor plants are ruined by frost. *S. azurea* is a good summer-flowering, blue-flowered species, and *S. leucantha* is valuable in November to December when its mauve and grey racemes are so welcome. All of these plants are grown under similar conditions to chrysanthemums, and, except *S. azurea*, are kept out of doors until frost threatens to cause damage.

41. *Solanum capsicastrum* in a 48 pot.

Solanum capsicastrum. One of the best subjects for Christmas decoration is the Winter Cherry (Plate 41). It is usually raised from seed sown February to March each year, but good forms are often propagated by cuttings. For this purpose the selected plant is cut back in January and the young shoots rooted as they become available, in a closed case. In either case they should be hardened off so that they may be plunged out of doors in May and kept there until frost is expected. If after fruiting they are good strong plants they can be lightly pruned and grown on for a second year. They do not like hot and dry situations, and will drop their foliage under these conditions: they are happiest in temperatures round 50° F. and with a reasonable amount of humidity.

91

Veronica. The late-flowering group of shrubby Veronicas or Hebes are valuable for a late autumn display. They are the easiest of plants to grow; in fact in favoured districts, particularly near the sea, they are hardy shrubs. They tend to become tall, and if retained for more than one year they require drastic pruning in early spring. Cuttings will root readily in a closed frame or propagating case, the best time for insertion being late summer. Of the *V. speciosa* varieties 'Veitchii' is a rich violet-purple, 'Simon Delaux' carmine, 'Gauntletti' pink, and 'Andersoni' lilac. Another useful plant of similar habit but different parentage is 'Blue Gem'.

The Lime Haters

The plants which follow are some of those which intensely dislike lime. Where the garden is on chalk and the water hard, the gardener is strongly advised to leave these alone, as, beautiful though they are, he will be everlastingly struggling against the insidious effects of lime, yellow foliage, unhappy plants, and so on.

Having disregarded the above, as he probably will, the only way is to pot up the plant in a special lime-free compost and to use only rain-water in watering. Easy to write but often difficult in practice!

It has always been recommended that these plants should be potted in a compost of two parts of peat to one of sand, but recent work at John Innes Institution* has proved that their J.I.S. Compost can be used successfully if the chalk is omitted and ¾ oz. of flowers of sulphur used in place; this compost is called J.I.S. (A). It has been used experimentally with ericas, one of the most difficult genera, and for the germination and cultivation of two species of rhododendron, and also for the rooting of cuttings of azaleas. These plants do not require high temperatures; in fact most of them only need to be kept frost-free. They are far healthier out of doors in summer and are best grown with the pots plunged in sharp ashes or sand which give good drainage, are firm enough to prevent the plants blowing over, and at the same time keep the roots cool and moist. With most of these

* *Journal of the Royal Horticultural Society*, vol. LXXX (1955).

42. Acacia, the florist's 'mimosa', at home on peach or vine wires.

plants hard ramming is the rule in potting, and overpotting must be avoided! Seeds are the easiest and best means of increase, but with most, cuttings of half-ripened shoots may be rooted in sharp sand in a propagating case.

Acacia. This is of course much better known as the 'Mimosa' of the florist. The one most frequently imported is *A. dealbata* (Plate 42), a native of Australia but now grown everywhere in the sub-tropics. It is almost hardy, in fact there are fine plants on the south coast and other favoured parts of Britain and most Fellows of The Royal Horticultural Society will be familiar with the specimen growing near the entrance to the Laboratories at Wisley. It is not easy to flower this species in a small house, as it is naturally a small tree and does not flower freely until it reaches a considerable size. A smaller and better species which is often trained on the wires of a greenhouse is *A. baileyana*. The flowers are similar but the foliage is smaller, neater, and silvery in colour. There are others rather different in character, but with the familiar fluffy yellow balls of flower, which are much more suitable for a greenhouse. The best for this purpose for pot cultivation is *A. armata* which has quite small entire leaves (strictly speaking, they are phyllodes), altogether unlike those of the 'Mimosa' of the florist. Even more unlike Mimosa in habit is *A. verticillata* with needle-like leaves, more like a conifer. This also with a little judicious pruning after flowering can be kept for some years in pots.

Callistemon. The 'Bottle Brush' trees are also of Australian origin. They are narrow leathery-leaved plants requiring light, dry, and sunny conditions. They are striking plants in flower, particularly those with crimson-scarlet inflorescences. They are evergreen and will thrive for years in pots; or where room is available, particularly head room (in lime-free soil) they may be planted in a greenhouse border to make large specimens. Potting, when required, should be done in March, and after flowering a light pruning will keep the plant compact and of reasonable size.

Pruning should not be done below the base of current year's wood or they may fail to 'break'. Plunging out of doors through the summer has the advantage of keeping the plants not only pest-free but compact in habit. The species, or rather the variety, most generally grown is *C. citrinus splendens*, in which the stamens are crimson (Plate 43).

Camellia. It is unfortunate that though these evergreen plants are hardy their beautiful flowers are so often ruined by spring frosts. Consequently if room can be found for them a little greenhouse protection while flowering will be well worth while. After flowering they can be hardened off and again plunged out of doors, preferably in part shade. There are a very wide range of varieties, both single and double, from which to select, and once a stock is obtained they are not difficult to propagate. For cultivation in pots careful watering is at all times necessary. To allow them to become 'bone dry' is often fatal and at the very least they will probably drop their buds and a year's crop may be lost.

Most varieties may be propagated by cuttings in a closed propagating case either in early spring or, with the current year's shoots, about August (see Propagation, page 72).

43. The brilliantly
    coloured flowers of
    callistemon are
    remarkably like the
    domestic bottle
    brush.

44. *Camellia japonica*
    'Adolphe Audus-
    son'. This fine
    semi-double variety
    is blood-red in
    colour with golden
    anthers.

45. *Camellia japonica* 'Alba Simplex'. In this single white variety the stamens stand out boldly.

The varieties most generally grown are those of *Camellia japonica*, of which there are single, double, anemone-formed, and paeony-formed flowers. Examples are 'Mathotiana' with red, pink, and white double flowers, and in single flowers, 'Alba Simplex', white (Plate 45), and 'Kimberley', red.

A new hybrid race raised by J. C. Williams in Cornwall about 1930 is called *C.* × *williamsii* and is rapidly becoming popular. Amongst the best are 'J. C. Williams' with soft pink single flowers, 'Mary Christian', similar but deeper in colour, and 'Donation' (Plate 46), also pale rose-pink and semi-double. The last was raised at Borde Hill in Sussex.

Ericas. At one time a large number of tender heaths were cultivated both as cool greenhouse plants and for market. They

46. 'Donation', one of the best varieties in the *Camellia × williamsii*
group; note the freedom of flowering in a pot-grown plant.

must be in a lime-free compost and are best grown on an ash
staging or bed of shingle which can be kept constantly moist,
though the plants must not be too wet. They do not at any time
require high temperatures, a 45° F. minimum being ample, but
to keep them compact and 'stocky' they should be as close as
possible to the glass. Shading is only required during hot sunshine. They can be out of doors from June to September, but
should be under cover before frost occurs. After flowering cut
the plants back; they may if required be repotted so soon as
growth commences or if in good condition merely top dressed.
Extremely careful watering is necessary throughout.

Propagation is not difficult; cuttings of young wood should
be inserted in June to July in pots of sandy peat in a propagating

D

47. A well-grown plant of *Erica hyemalis* in a 48 pot.

case at about 60° F. Six good species, all vigorous growers,
are *E. cavendishii*, *E. melanthera*, *E. gracilis* (Plate 48), *E.
pageana*, *E. hyemalis* (Plate 47), and *E. ventricosa*, and there are
also a number of varieties.

Rhododendrons. Rhododendron is a huge genus which can provide
a wealth of material either for alpine or cool greenhouse, and
either hardy plants lifted from the open for gentle forcing or
tender plants grown in pots and brought under glass for the
winter.

Cultivation is much the same for all. They may be brought

48. *Erica gracilis*, of lighter, more graceful habit.

into the greenhouse when the buds begin to swell, but the cooler they are grown the longer will be the life of the flowers. After flowering they should be kept warm and growing freely to build up the plant and flower buds for the following year. In June they can be plunged out of doors preferably in a cool, half-shady situation. They must never be allowed to dry out completely. When they are really dry it is worth while watering by immersion in a bucket or tank.

One of the worst pests is red spider, especially in a hot, dry summer; frequent syringing, or hosing if the water is soft, is

49. The wonderful freedom of flowering of Rhododendron
   'Fragrantissimum'.

the best means of prevention, and should control be necessary
syringe with H.E.T.P.

In the days of the large conservatory no garden was complete
without some of the tender species and varieties of *Rhododendron*.
Now, except for favoured localities where they can be
grown out of doors, they have practically dropped out of
cultivation. Three at least of these fine old hybrids are still
grown, however, 'Countess of Haddington', 'Lady Alice
Fitzwilliam', and 'Fragrantissimum' (Plate 49). In all three the
flowers are white, tinged with pink, and fragrant. They are
excellent pot plants and wonderfully free-flowering even when
quite small. Among the species *R. lindleyi* (Plate 50) and *R.
taggianum* have very large lily-like white flowers and make
good plants for the larger cool greenhouse.

100

50. *Rhododendron lindleyi* with lovely white fragrant flowers. A species from the Himalayas.

The evergreen group better known as 'Indian' Azaleas mainly derived from *R. simsii* are too well known to need description. They provide a wonderful range of colour in single and double varieties (Plate 51). Strong plants should be purchased in autumn and potted firmly in peat and lime-free loam. They should be grown cool, preferably without heat, a deep cold frame being sufficient if 'matted' during frost.

The many beautiful varieties of *R. obtusum*, best known as Kurume Azaleas, are also first-rate pot plants for early spring flowering and can be treated in the same way.

51. A bank of 'Indian' azaleas in pots. Note the protection of polythene lining. This will keep out several degrees of frost.

5 · Tender Herbaceous Plants and Sub-shrubs

These generally require a somewhat higher temperature and a greater degree of humidity. It is, of course, a great deal more expensive to keep up a higher winter minimum temperature, but when a 50° F. minimum can be maintained there is a considerable increase in the range of plants which may be grown.

Begonia is a huge and very diverse genus, and species may be brought into flower right through the year. *B. rex* is a group of beautiful ornamental-leaved varieties with a wonderful range of colour and shades (Plate 52). They do best in fairly heavy shade and will in fact usually do well under the staging of a light greenhouse. With this group it is best to keep vigorous young stock and discard old plants. They are easily propagated by means of leaf cuttings or they may be increased by stem cuttings or division of the old plant preferably in early summer. They are grown by firms who specialize in 'house' plants, but the easy way to build up a stock is to beg a leaf from fellow gardeners and propagate from it.

Beloperone guttata, the shrimp plant, is one of the best greenhouse plants of fairly recent introduction. Its inflorescences are handsome and long-lasting, the white flowers are short-lived, and the really conspicuous part is the red or bronze bracts, which remain on the plant an incredibly long time. The plant is easily propagated by means of cuttings.

Coleus have again become popular for their diversity of colour and form. They are all forms of one species, *C. blumei*, but they provide an amazing range of foliage colour from green through yellow and red to maroon. Though named varieties are still perpetuated by cuttings, coleus are being raised from seed annually in increasing numbers.

Cuttings should be inserted in autumn; young shoots 2 to 3 inches long are best. They quickly root and are much more

52. Varieties of *Begonia rex* showing the wonderful diversity in form and tone within this group.

readily carried through the winter than are old plants. For seedlings seed is sown thinly in pans or boxes in February or March and sown in a minimum temperature of 60°F. Pot off as early as possible in J.I.P.$_1$. into 60's or into boxes if a number are grown. Some growers discard all green seedlings, but it is as well to grow some on for a while as it is difficult to judge them so small. Move when ready into 48's, using J.I.P.$_2$. If tall plants are desired they may be allowed to grow, but it is usually better to keep them bushy by repeated pinching out of the terminal shoots, and later of the lateral shoots until it forms a rounded bushy plant. Flowers are always pinched out. They respond to generous weekly feeding from 48-size pots. The temperature need not be high, 55°F. being sufficient, but they must not be allowed to dry out and are better shaded in bright sunshine. Three good named varieties are 'Diane', red with green edging, 'Pompadour', red, green, and cream, 'Vesuvius', red with gold edging. *C. thyrsoideus* and *C. frederici* are grown as flowering plants and valued for their deep blue panicles of flowers

53. Gloxinias, a bench of well-grown plants showing an extensive range of colour.

which are produced in winter. Cuttings will become available in February to March and can easily be rooted in a propagating case. When rooted they should be potted off singly and grown on near the glass to keep them stocky, pinching out the laterals to make a compact bush.

Gloxinias are amongst the most colourful of greenhouse plants for summer and early autumn (Plate 53). They are not worth while attempting unless a winter temperature of at least 50° F. is being maintained. They look exotic but in fact are no more difficult than many other plants, the essentials for cultivation being a warm, moist house, shading during bright sunshine, and a light, well-drained compost. Named varieties are not much grown today because if a batch of plants is raised from seed of a good strain a few of the best can be selected for propagation. Alternatively, dormant tubers can be bought and started into growth about January, for July flowering, or a month or so later for autumn display. Seeds are extremely fine and need as much care in sowing as begonias. If sown January to

105

February they should flower the same year; if in June, the following year. They may also be propagated by means of leaf cuttings. These are cut with $\frac{1}{2}$ to 1 inch of stalk which is inserted in sandy compost in the cutting frame. They will soon form small tubers which may remain dormant until the following spring.

Impatiens gives us both annual and perennial species suitable for the greenhouse. The best of the perennials for pots are *I. holstii* and *I. sultani*, the former orange in colour and the latter scarlet. Many intermediate colour forms are grown. Though they require a reasonably high temperature in winter they will do out of doors during the summer. They are quick-growing, easily propagated by means of cuttings, and almost continuous flowering. Less common but an excellent greenhouse plant is *I. oliveri*. It is a larger plant than the others with pale lilac flowers. This group of plants should not be too liberally treated, as they flower more freely if somewhat starved. They are often known as Water Fuchsia or Water Balsam.

Peperomias are old-established plants in gardens but are now making a comeback as house plants. One of the best known is *P. glabella*, with heart-shaped deep green leaves, pink fleshy stems, and a trailing habit of growth. Another popular one is *P. sandersi argyreia*, which is more erect in habit and has leaves marked with silver between the veins. For the greenhouse a much greater range is available, as they thrive in warm, humid conditions. They are, however, best in part shade.

Plumbago rosea and its white variety are easy to grow and free-flowering, and useful especially for autumn and winter. In February or March, cuttings can be inserted and when rooted potted off singly. When growing freely stop them by pinching out the leading growths and again when they have made about 3 to 5 inches of new growth. Keep them close to the glass, as they tend to become straggly in habit.

Saintpaulia ionantha, popularly known as African violet, is too well known to need description. They do best in a warm house until they reach flowering size when they can be kept cooler. Given free drainage and careful watering, cultivation is easy. There is now an extremely wide range of varieties in all shades

54. Saintpaulia, a well-flowered plant of a single variety.

55. One of the double-flowered varieties of Saintpaulia, 'Melior Pink'.

of blue and violet and good clear pinks and whites (Plates 54 and 55). Seed is extremely fine and needs similar treatment to that of begonias. Stocks can also be increased both by division of the old plants and leaf cuttings. In fact propagation by this means has become so common that it is not unusual to buy leaves of the named varieties to root at home. Though African it is not a violet but closely related to *Streptocarpus* and gloxinia.

Strelitzia reginae always excites admiration when bearing those striking blue and yellow flowers which suggest the name Crane flower (Plate 56). They are vigorous plants about 4 feet high, and are better planted in a sunny border in the greenhouse if possible. Pot cultivation is not difficult, but it is a vigorous grower and will probably require a 9- or 10-inch pot before it will flower.

It must have sunshine, and in fact fits in well with succulent plants. From spring to autumn it may be watered liberally, but during the winter careful watering is essential. It will tolerate winter temperatures as low as 45° F., but better results are obtained with a higher minimum. It may be divided in spring or, if seed can be obtained, it can easily be raised from seed.

Ferns

Ferns are a group which are usually better kept by themselves so that they can be given the shady and humid conditions on which they thrive. There are an enormous number and an infinite variety from hardy to tropical and from an inch or two in height to the huge tree ferns of New Zealand. Cultivation is much the same for all. They resent too strong light and sunshine and many will promptly lose their fronds if too exposed. Potting and division should be done early in the year, February for choice, before the new growth begins to develop. They will do quite well in John Innes Compost, but should have rather better drainage than is usual. They should never be allowed to become really dry while growing, though a little drier through the winter. They should stand on gravel, shingle, or ashes, which can be kept constantly damped where possible, and floors and brickwork should also be damped freely to keep up a humid atmosphere.

56. *Strelitzia reginae*, the Crane flower, also known as Bird of Paradise flower. The Latin name is in honour of Queen Charlotte.

In addition to propagation by division all ferns may be raised from spores, which are of course the equivalent of seeds in flowering plants. Spores should be sown either on sterilized soil or on peat which is reasonably sterile, covered by a sheet of glass and kept shaded. The whole surface will first become green and then what are called prothalli develop, followed after a time by tiny fern fronds. When these are large enough to handle, prick out patches of them on to new soil and grow them on in shade and humidity. The pans are often stood in clay saucers with an inch or so of water to ensure that they remain constantly moist.

For our present purpose it will be sufficient to refer to those which will thrive reasonably well in a mixed temperate greenhouse, though preferably in a shady corner.

Adiantums, the maidenhair ferns, are quite easy and too well known to need a description. Most of them have rhizomes which render propagation by division easy. This should be done about February before new growth is too advanced. Alternatively, they can be raised from spores. *A. capillus-veneris* is one of the hardiest and will do well with a minimum of 40° F. Another easy one is *A. cuneatum* which is vigorous, easy to increase, and one of the best for cutting for floral work. Somewhat different in habit, but equally easy and accommodating, is the New Zealand group of which *A. diaphanum* and *A. hispidulum* are typical.

Asplenium bulbiferum is well known, and is one of the best examples of a plant which bears living young on its fronds. Its propagation is simplicity itself, you merely detach the young plant from the old frond and pot it.

Davallia is one of the most graceful with very finely pinnatified (or feathery) fronds. This runs about freely by rhizomes and again division is no problem. Two easy ones are *D. bullata* and *D. canariensis*.

Nephrolepis. One of the most popular and graceful of all genera is *Nephrolepis*, the hardiest being *N. exaltata*, the ladder fern, with long arching but not pinnatified fronds. Two of the really cristate forms are *N. todaeoides* and *N. marshallii*, but they are not quite so easy.

Pteris. Almost hardy and amongst the easiest are *Pteris*, especially *P. cretica* and its numerous varieties, the best known of which is probably *albolineata*, and the crested form 'Wimsettii'. *P. tremula* is much larger and an excellent greenhouse fern which also has crested and feathery forms.

Platycerium bifurcatum is a striking plant producing fronds of two different types. The sterile fronds are roundish and designed for clasping the limbs of trees or similar support and the fertile or spore-bearing fronds are drooping and divided; the spores being borne at the end of these divisions. It is best grown wired on to a board, a piece of old tree fern, or cork bark, and a ball of porous orchid compost packed round the roots. It does best in shade and must never be allowed to become too dry.

A tough leathery-leaved species is the holly fern *Cyrtomium* (or *Aspidium*) *falcatum*. Quite different in habit is *Lomaria gibba* which makes a trunk up to 2 or 3 feet and is in fact a miniature tree fern. True tree ferns such as *Dicksonias* want too much room both vertically and laterally.

Selaginellas. These are flowerless plants closely allied to true ferns. They are equally as fond of moisture and grow well under the same conditions as ferns. Most of them are also shade-loving, but some will tolerate sunshine and a few take on vivid foliage colours under these conditions.

A number of species like quite cool conditions, one, in particular, *S. kraussiana*, being almost hardy. They are easily increased either by division of the clumps or by cuttings. I have always found that small cuttings eventually make better plants than divided plants. For a cool house the two best are the one just mentioned, *S. kraussiana*, and *S. uncinata*; for slightly warmer conditions *S. caulescens* is good. There are plenty of others, but they do require somewhat warmer conditions.

57. A view of the Temperate House at Wisley showing the use made of climbing plants.

6 · Climbing Plants

The term climbing plants will include all plants suitable for clothing walls, roof, wires, etc. Generally the amateur has too small a structure for him to use to advantage the more vigorous climbing plants, and in giving the following selection it is not for one moment suggested that he should overload his greenhouse with climbers. There is, however, such a wealth of available plants that it is a pity not to find room for one or two either to train over the roof, or in the case of three-quarter-span or lean-to houses, on the back wall of his house. Many climbing plants can be grown in pots and either trained round four canes or over the old-fashioned but valuable 'balloon' wire framework. In this case they can often be placed out of doors in summer if not in flower.

Too often the amateur's greenhouse contains none at all. Yet they can provide a living background or framework in the same way as a planting of shrubs or conifers can do in the open garden. Plants of climbing habit have the advantage that they furnish the upper part of the house, and incidentally provide some shade in summer when most needed, and yet leave plenty of room below (Plate 57). There are plants suitable whether the house be warm or cold, and it is well worth while experimenting with some of the less common plants.

With some of these there is quite a good deal of tying necessary, but with others, if trellis or wires are provided, they will take advantage of these and give little trouble.

For a small house with a minimum of 45° F. I would suggest *Jasminum polyanthum* for a winter flowering and *Passiflora coerulea* or its variety 'Constance Elliott' for summer, while for a late-flowering species I would suggest *Solanum jasminoides*. Where tying-in is necessary, trellis work is an advantage; the shoots can be woven into the trellis to some extent without tying.

Abutilons, though not strictly climbers, are excellent subjects for training on pillars and roof wires and the pendulous flowers are seen to best advantage from below. There is an excellent colour

58. *Abutilon milleri*. This is small enough and hardy enough for any frost-free greenhouse.

range. The pure white 'Boule de Neige' is an old but good one, so also the two yellows, 'Canary Bird' and 'Golden Fleece'; and for a deep red, 'Red Ashfold'. For a small house the Brazilian species *A. megapotamicum* is useful. Its flowers are red and yellow and borne right through the summer where the plant is happy. It is rarely more than 6 or 8 feet in height. Similar and equally useful is *A. milleri* (Plate 58).

Cobaea scandens is an unusual plant from South America with pinnate leaves and tendrils at the tips. The flowers are in shape like some of the cup-and-saucer Canterbury bells. They open

59. *Cobaea scandens* can easily be raised from seed to flower the same year. A quick-growing plant for the impatient gardener.

bright green and at maturity become violet (Plate 59). There is also a white variety.

Eccremocarpus scaber, the 'Glory Flower' of Chile, is easily raised from seed and will flower the first year. It has light graceful foliage and racemes of pleasing orange-red tubular flowers, or yellow in the case of the variety *aurea*.

Fuchsia. In the old-fashioned, roomy conservatories, the fuchsia was a valuable and popular plant. It was trained not only in bush and standard form but also tied in to wires on the pillars and roofs. For this and for baskets it is well adapted, as the suspended flowers look well from below. For this purpose specimens are selected and trained up on one lead by pinching outside growths until the eaves of the house are reached, from then as many growths can be allowed as there are wires to tie them to. They are then allowed to make natural growth in summer, but are spurred back to the main branches in winter. Planted in a border and grown in this way they will remain in good condition for years.

Vigorous growing varieties are of course best, and there are plenty to choose from. I still like 'Rose of Castille', 'Ballet Girl', and 'Phenomenal'.

One of the South American species, *F. corymbiflora*, is seen at its best against a wall or pillar; it is 10 or 12 feet in height with bold foliage and huge clusters of long scarlet pendulous flowers, followed later by shining maroon-coloured fruits.

Gloriosas. The Glory lilies are tuberous-rooted climbers closely related to true lilies. They are rested and kept dry during the winter months and started into growth about February or March. They will do quite well in a cool greenhouse, but do require plenty of humidity. *G. superba* is probably the easiest and has flowers of orange and red during the summer. There is also a yellow variety. The most brilliant is *G. rothschildiana* with crimson flowers. They are slow-growing if raised from seed, but if tubers are obtained while dormant they should flower the first season. These are said to need tropical temperatures, but we have flowered them for many years in a house without fire heat from June to September.

Jasminum. There are two species of jasmines which are particularly valuable for the cool greenhouse.

In *J. polyanthum* the flowers, though pink in bud, are a clear wax-like white and beautifully fragrant. It is at its best in February or early March. It will climb readily over wires and is self-supporting. It is a very rampant grower (Plate 60). The other is best known as *J. primulinum* though its correct name is now *J. mesnyi*. The flowers are yellow but lacking the fragrance of *J. polyanthum*. It also requires more care and attention, as it does not climb and has to be tied in. It is also spring-flowering.

116

60. *Jasminum polyanthum*, a sweetly scented species valuable in late winter. It may either be planted in a border or pot grown.

Both these plants may be grown out of doors in the milder parts of the country, but in other districts are excellent cool house plants. If grown as pot plants they can be cut over after flowering and plunged out of doors for the summer months; for this purpose they are best trained round tall canes.

Hoya carnosa is an evergreen climber which produces close clusters of beautifully symmetrical pink wax-like flowers (Plate 61). It is easily grown in a cool greenhouse and when in flower is a great favourite as a house plant. For this purpose it must, of course, be kept in pots and trained balloon fashion over wires or canes. *H. bella* is a smaller plant with pure white flowers and violet centres. It requires warmer conditions and is sometimes grafted on to *H. carnosa* to increase its vigour.

Lapageria rosea is one of the most beautiful of climbing plants, with pendulous bell-shaped, wax-like flowers (Plate 62), allied to the lilies.

61. *Hoya carnosa* is best grown in pots.

62. *Lapageria rosea*, the national flower of Chile, an excellent cool house plant.

It is excellent for a cool greenhouse or cold house, especially where soil is on the acid side and the water soft. Where the water is hard the best way is to grow it in peat and sand, and so far as is possible to use only rain-water. The type is rosy pink, and there is an excellent white form and several other varieties. The most practical method of propagation is by layering, unless seed can be obtained. The worst enemy of this plant is the slug, which vastly enjoys the young emerging shoots, and will apparently travel any distance to get them.

Pelargoniums. Some of the Zonal Pelargoniums (geraniums) may be used for furnishing walls, etc., up to 6 or 8 feet if grown on without stopping and can be floriferous if given plenty of light and air and good compost. The ivy-leaved varieties are also well suited to the purpose, and though not of much value for their flowers some of the scented-leaved species such as *P. radula* 'climb' freely. 'Chlorinda' and 'Pretty Polly' are exceptions in that they are decorative and free-flowering as well as scented-leaved.

Petrea volubilis is a vigorous twining plant with long racemes of violet and blue flowers. It does well under quite cool conditions and is in my experience best grown in pots with the growth tied in round canes or a wire framework.

Pharbitis (Ipomoea). The convolvulus family provides us with a number of useful climbers, in this case with twining stems.

The most beautiful is the annual ' Morning Glory ', now called *Pharbitis tricolor* but better known as *Ipomoea rubro-coerulea* or *I. tricolor*. There are few flower colours to equal this plant for purity of blue, but unfortunately the flowers are short-lived and are usually gone towards evening. It is a vigorous climber and is best on wires, though it may be trained round three canes. Its lovely blue flowers are worth the effort of tying in and training.

'Morning Glories' are not too easy to transplant and it is worth while sowing about three seeds in a 5-inch pot and, when these are large enough, moving on to an 8-inch pot without transplanting at all.

Plumbago capensis. The South African leadwort is attractive whether grown as a pot plant or planted and trained over a trellis or wires (Plate 63). Both the pale blue species and its white variety are free-flowering and were at one time extremely popular plants. A winter minimum of 45° F. is sufficient, but plants should be kept on the dry side until March. It should be pruned fairly hard when repotting as the flowers are borne on the young growths. Cuttings are easily rooted in late summer.

Rhodochiton volubile is easily raised from seed and will flower within the year if sown early. It has dark purple flowers which fall away when mature, and light purple calyxes which remain decorative for a long period.

Solanums. Several species of this genus may be used for greenhouse work. *S. jasminoides* is light and graceful in foliage and free-flowering. It is naturally of climbing habit and, though it can be grown out of doors in the milder parts of Britain, is in most gardens better in a cool house. The species is pale blue or lilac, but many gardeners prefer the white variety. Much

120

63. *Plumbago capensis* is summer-flowering, and if pot grown can be used out of doors from June to September.

more vigorous and imposing, though more tender, is *S. wendlandii* from Costa Rica. The foliage is deep bright green and the immense trusses of flowers are lilac to blue. It is only recommended for large houses as it can grow to 20 feet. In the colder parts of the country the Chilean *S. crispum* may be worth growing under glass, though in milder districts it will succeed on a sheltered wall out of doors.

Streptosolen jamesonii was at one time extremely popular but is not so well known today. It is related to the solanums and hails from Colombia. The orange-coloured flowers are borne freely from June onwards. Kept to a single leader it will reach 8 feet or more in height.

7 · Plants Raised from Seed

Plants raised from seed may include annuals, biennials, and even short-lived perennials, anything in fact that will provide a colourful display in season and at a reasonable cost. The present popularity of this type of plant is without doubt partly due to wartime fuel control and later its price. Another important factor is the practical demonstrations of what can be achieved with them which annually appear at flower shows throughout the country.

Those who have had the pleasure of seeing the wonderful groups staged at Chelsea Flower Show each year will realize that this is no exaggeration. Year by year new and improved selections are shown of an immense range of plants most of which can easily be grown in a cool greenhouse. Most of the annual and biennial groups of plants do best under cool, airy conditions and only require sufficient heat to exclude frost. Most of them are better without heat from April onwards.

The two main periods of sowing are August to October for wintering under glass and from January onwards for those plants which do not winter well. From the autumn sowings we can expect a spring display and from January and successional sowings we can follow on with batches to carry us right through the rest of the year. The period from November to February is the difficult time. Careful watering and maximum possible light are equally necessary, the best possible situation being shelves near the glass.

At all times sowing should be thin, as the most likely trouble is damping off. Prick off at the earliest possible moment for the same reason. While seedlings are usually pricked out singly with some annuals such as nemesia and *Phlox drummondii*, better results are obtained if three seedlings are pricked off round the rim of the 60-size pot. When these are moved on they will merge into one and give a fuller effect than single plants. With most seedlings some support will be necessary. Twigs from an old birch broom are good if the plants are allowed to grow through

64. A colourful and diverse group consisting mainly of plants raised from seed. Note the 'Morning Glory' on the roof.

and over them, or alternatively thin bamboo canes and neat tying will give sufficient support.

To list alphabetically all the plants suitable for this purpose would require more space than is available and there are several good books on annuals which do this. All I can do is to glance over the seasons and suggest a few of the most suitable. These are arranged roughly in the order in which they will flower.

In the early months of the New Year bulbs are so largely grown that generally only a limited number of other plants are required. Available, however, are some of the most useful and decorative of pot-grown plants; for example, cyclamen, primulas, and cinerarias.

Calendula, the Pot Marigold, is one of the easiest and most reliable for flowering early in the New Year (Plate 65). Sowing should be done in August so that fair-sized plants can be built up before winter. 'Radio' is a popular variety with rich orange flowers, and for contrast either 'Lemon Queen' or the cream 'Twilight'.

Cyclamen persicum (Plate 66) is a native of the Eastern Mediterranean. It is light, graceful, and fragrantly flowered, in many shades of pink to white. From it have been developed, by patient breeding and selection, the large flowered races of many colours, the cyclamen of the florist.

Cyclamen are raised annually in thousands for the market. The seeds are relatively large and easily handled, and the usual method is to sow an inch or so apart in boxes from August onwards in cold frames. Little growth is made before autumn and they are usually left in seed boxes until February to March, though they should be brought into the greenhouse in October. They are grown on steadily under cool conditions until July, when they are potted into 5- or 6-inch pots in J.I.P.$_3$. Care must be taken not to pot too deeply; most of the corm should be above the soil surface. They want shade from strong sunshine, but otherwise as much light as possible, or they may become drawn and spoiled.

Careful watering at all times is essential, and a fair amount of atmospheric humidity. Feed every fourteen days during the summer. Syringing will help to keep down red spider which can be troublesome. If it does get a hold, use an azobenzine fumigating cone. These are made in various sizes for houses or frames of different capacity.

If they are of first-class quality the corms can be kept and grown on. After flowering they should be gradually ripened off and rested until August, then soaked and repotted. They can, if desired, be retained for several years, in fact they have been known to live for thirty years, but it is generally accepted that young vigorous plants are best.

65. Calendula is one
of the easiest of
annuals to carry
through the winter
for early flowering.

66. *Cyclamen persicum.*
The species is, as
the photograph
shows, not only
graceful but
wonderfully free-
flowering.

67. Cyclamen. A typical plant of an up-to-date strain. They now have a wide range of colour from white through pink and lilac to purple.

Primula. No genus of plants is more variable than the winter-flowering Primulas. The toughest is *P. obconica*, which also has a long flowering season (Plate 68). Its large heads of flowers may be lilac through pink and mauve shades to maroon. The great handicap of this plant is that many people are allergic to it and it can, on those unfortunate people, cause a most unpleasant and irritating skin rash.

P. malacoides is altogether more graceful, with smaller foliage and compact spikes of flowers (Plate 69). Until recent years only shades of lilac were available, but today they can be obtained in a wonderful range of colours, in fact in all shades of lilac, rich pink to crimson and maroon, or, if desired, white. They are almost hardy and will tolerate quite low temperatures so long as frost is excluded.

P. sinensis also has an immense range of varieties and a good colour range (Plate 70). This species is interesting in that it is not known wild. It has been cultivated in China for centuries and was introduced from Canton in 1820.

68. *Primula obconica*
is one of the most
reliable of winter-
flowering plants
for the greenhouse.

69. *Primula malacoides*
may be obtained in
a wide range of
colours and shades.

127

70. *Primula sinensis* has also been much improved in recent years.

It is somewhat strange that the yellow-flowered *P. kewensis* has not become more popular as a pot plant. It is no more difficult to grow and is most striking when in flower, while it is as hardy as the other species. This is a plant of garden origin raised at Kew, and for many years it had to be propagated vegetatively as it produced no seed. Then quite suddenly a fertile plant arose which produced good seed and rendered its cultivation easy.

Primulas are by no means difficult to grow and only require a greenhouse or frame which can be kept above 45° F. in winter. *P. obconica* and *P. sinensis* should be sown under glass in May or June, and *P. malacoides* a month or so later. Care is necessary in handling the seeds, as they are very small. The seed pots should be covered with glass and paper until germination takes place and pricked off at the earliest possible moment preferably into 3-inch pots. At this season no artificial heat should be necessary and they should be grown as cool as possible and given plenty of air. In late summer they will be ready for a move into 5-inch pots and they will usually make good plants and flower in this size. From early October they require protection and will benefit from a little artificial heat, though they never need more than 45° F. to 50° F.

Quite a number of plants may be grown in nursery lines in the garden until autumn and then lifted and potted. Amongst the best are the double-flowered wallflower; the winter-flowering strains of pansies; polyanthus and primrose in many colours and shades. Early flowering primulas such as *P. denticulata* and *P. rosea* also give a good return for very little trouble and so do the old-fashioned auriculas.

Cinerarias as grown today are entirely plants of garden origin and have been to a very great extent developed by British raisers. They are woody perennials, though most of the garden races are treated as tender biennials.

For winter flowering they should be sown in April and, for later batches, in June.

During the summer months the cooler they can be grown the better, and a cool, shaded frame or greenhouse is best. From September onwards they should have a little artificial heat and most careful watering is essential.

There are many different strains or selections, but they come into three main groups:

1. Multiflora. These are large flowered, usually of dwarf compact habit, and either in self colours or bicolours.
2. Stellata. Taller growing and with much smaller flowers borne in profusion.
3. Intermediates which combine to a varying degree the characters of both.

There is a wonderful selection of colours either in selfs or mixed.

The worst pest is greenfly and constant watch is necessary. Leaf miner also can be troublesome.

Other plants readily raised from seed are the 'Annual' types of carnation and stocks (Plate 71). Both these require a long season of growth. Stocks to flower in January should be sown not later than June and grown as cool as possible to keep them sturdy.

129

E

71. Stocks. The most important points in the cultivation of winter-
flowering stocks are to obtain the best possible strains and to grow
them as cool as possible.

Antirrhinums. For spring display *Antirrhinum* can provide a good and effective range of colour and height. They should be over-wintered in 3-inch pots in protected cold frames and moved into 5-inch pots in January, transferring into the greenhouse. Light colours are usually best and for most purposes inter-mediate varieties. 'Romance' is a lovely pink and 'Amber Queen' and 'Apricot Queen' both good.

Calceolaria. During spring the harvest is reaped of the late summer and autumn sowings which have been carefully pro-tected and guarded throughout the winter. Probably the most spectacular genus is *Calceolaria* which alone can provide an infinite range of colour and variety.

There are many different strains on the market and before attempting to grow them it is as well to study their respective merits. Self colours can now be obtained, but most strains are of multicoloured forms. Many of the large-flowered types are amongst the most vivid of greenhouse plants. At the other extreme are the graceful small-flowered strains in which the flowers are borne in sprays up to 2 feet high. To flower from April onwards they should be sown in June. The seed is fine and dust-like and needs careful treatment (see Chapter 3, page 70). Prick out at the earliest possible moment and pot on as required, keeping the plants cool and humid. They can re-main in cold frames until mid-October, when they should be given the lightest possible position in the greenhouse. In February they will need moving into their 6- or 7-inch final pots. Throughout the winter very careful watering is necessary; if too wet, fungoid diseases can cause casualties. Fumigation should also be done periodically to check aphis. These plants are not easy to grow and the novice would be wiser to try his hand at the shrubby group which is easier.

The common Canterbury bell is also an excellent pot plant and may be grown in a good range of colours. These are often lifted from the nursery rows in autumn and potted. Wintered in cold frames they will flower in April and May.

Summer is, of course, the peak time for annuals, and there is an enormous range available from which to select. A further advantage is that no artificial heating is required. Two of the best genera for this period are *Schizanthus* and *Salpiglossis* in a bewildering range of colours and shades.

Schizanthus. Probably the most widely and successfully grown of all pot plants is *Schizanthus* (Plate 72). There are many distinct strains available differing in shape, size of flower, and range of colour, and it is worth while going to some trouble to select a good strain. Its culture is not difficult, but it does repay care and attention as well as any plant. Seed may be sown from August onwards and the seedlings should be pricked out either into boxes or small pots until about November, when they should be moved into the 3-inch pots in which they will remain until February or March. (Refer to notes on pricking out, page 42.) The final potting into J.I.P.$_2$ may be into 7- or 8-inch pots.

They should be kept cool, and reasonably dry atmospheric conditions are desirable in winter. They are quite safe at 40° F., or even 35° F., provided they have been grown hard; that is, given ample ventilation and light. Staking is essential and thin bamboo canes are the most suitable; height depends on the strain, some will reach 4 or 5 feet. They are subject to fungus diseases during winter, so that very damp conditions and deep potting of the seedlings should be avoided. If desired, they can be pushed along to flower from April onwards.

Salpiglossis sinuata. It is curious that this species and *Schizanthus* may be found growing together in the wild in Chile. They are excellent in combination, the relatively small 'butterflies' of the *Schizanthus* contrasting with the larger trumpets of *Salpiglossis*. This species gives us some of the most brilliant colours in horticulture and in the pencilling of one colour on another there is nothing quite like them (Plate 73). It is one of the more difficult plants to carry through the winter and due allowance must be made for losses. For the novice I should advise leaving them until he has gained experience and skill. January sowing in heat avoids this difficulty, but the results are not so good as with autumn sowing.

72. Schizanthus. Few genera can show greater diversity in colour and marking. Its light, airy flowers have earned it the name Butterfly flower.

73. Salpiglossis is remarkable for the colour contrasts it produces and the delicate marking and pencilling of one colour on another.

Begonias. There is now a good selection of varieties of the fibrous-rooted begonias. Though these are really perennial they may be raised from seed sown in February and March for summer flowering. Colours available range from pure white through pinks to crimson and they will flower well into autumn. An excellent pair are 'White Queen' and 'Indian Maid', the latter with scarlet flowers and deep bronze foliage; another striking variety is 'Frosted Chocolate', with dark foliage and white flowers. Plants which have been used for bedding purposes, if lifted carefully and potted, will often continue to flower under glass right into winter.

Godetia is popular for summer flowering and there are some lovely shades now available. **Phlox drummondii** also provides an excellent colour range and has a relatively long-flowering period.

Kochia. The summer cypress is erect in habit and as the common name suggests resembles a small conifer. It is excellent for breaking up strong colour contrasts. It is best raised from February onwards as it is difficult to winter successfully.

Nemesia now offers a beautiful range of brilliant colours; gold, crimson, and red, or blue, yellow, and white.

For later in the year, July onwards, the more tender annuals may be used. 'Cockscombs' or *Celosia* are perhaps best known, and both the cristate type and the plumose are good. Torenias, both lilac and yellow, are equally useful and a good blue-flowered greenhouse annual is *Exacum affine*. It will not be necessary to sow these until March or April as they want quick growing in warm conditions.

Late Summer and Early Autumn

Browallia speciosa is in fact a perennial, but it is usually treated as an annual and raised from seed in spring. It is one of the best blue-flowering plants and an excellent pot plant. It can also be used for flowering in winter.

Campanulas. Of the biennial group the best known and generally useful is the Chimney campanula, *C. pyramidalis*. Its tall spires of blue and white, 4 to 6 feet in height, are most valuable in the summer and autumn. For this purpose they should be raised

134

from seed in summer, potted into 5-inch pots about September, and grown in protected cold frames through the winter. About March to April they may be potted on into the 8- or 9-inch pots in which they will flower. They may be plunged out of doors, preferably in a bed of ashes, from April until the buds are well advanced.

Another campanula which may be grown under identical conditions, though it is not quite so hardy, is *C. vidalii*. It is a species from the Azores of bushy habit with white bell-shaped drooping flowers borne in July and August.

Salvia. For greenhouse use there are a considerable number of species available and some of those grown for bedding purposes, such as the scarlet *S. splendens* and the blue *S. patens*, are valuable. Both were formerly propagated vegetatively, but as the varieties now come true from seed this is no longer necessary.

Plants are raised in spring, grown on in cold frames through the summer, and potted on when required. They are kept pinched to keep them bushy and flower buds nipped off until September. They will flower right through autumn and early winter with a minimum temperature of 50°F.

Streptocarpus, the 'Cape Primroses', are well within the limits of the small greenhouse. They are delightful plants and have been tremendously improved in recent years. From two sowings in succession, plants may be brought in to flower from May to October. For early work sow in July and carry through the winter in 3-inch pots, potting on into 5-inch pots about March. For later work a January or February sowing will make nice plants to follow the first batch. Seed is dust-like and needs extreme care. A propagating case is almost essential.

It is doubtful whether it is worth while to carry on plants into the second year, though if a plant is exceptionally good it can be easily perpetuated by leaf cuttings as is done with the named varieties.

Trachelium coeruleum is an excellent plant for the cool house. Though naturally a perennial it is usually treated as an annual or biennial (Plate 74). If sown in July strong plants can be built up for flowering the following summer. They can be

74. *Trachelium coeruleum* is almost hardy and only requires protection from frost.

frame-grown until October when they are best in the green-house.

The very word autumn brings to mind chrysanthemums, and even here there is a wonderful range of varieties which may be raised from seed. Two of the best are the 'Charm' group (Plate 113) and the 'Cascade' (Plate 114).

The Marguerite carnations are a valuable race for autumn flowering. Sown about February, they should be grown as cool as possible and hardened off in spring for cultivation either in the open or cold frames. At all times they must have plenty of light and air.

Capsicum annuum. For autumn colour the decorative fruits of the 'Chile Pepper', *C. annuum*, are striking and unusual.

There are many varieties having fruits of various shapes and sizes, some erect on the branches, others pendulous, and providing different shades of scarlet, red, and yellow. They are raised from seed sown under glass in spring. If you save your own seed treat it with care. The fruits are peppery, and if the irritant reaches the eyes it is painful. For December and Christmas decoration also there is the closely related ornamental-fruited *Solanum capsicastrum*.

So once again we come back to the valuable primulas and cyclamen.

Climbing Plants from Seed

The 'Morning Glory' is one of the most beautiful of annuals. It is described on p. 120 and is best grown annually from seed.

Maurandia. Though strictly speaking these are perennials they are usually treated as annuals and sown early under glass. Sown about the end of February and potted on when ready, they will give an excellent account of themselves either grown on wires or round stakes. They climb naturally by means of the leaf petioles which twist themselves round wires, twigs, or other support. The most generally grown species is *M. barclaiana* which provides a range of colour from purple through lavender to rose and white. *M. scandens* is very similar and *M. erubescens* has much larger rose-pink glandular flowers.

Thunbergia alata is another worthwhile annual climber from South Africa. Its flowers vary in colour through white, fawn, and yellow, the most striking form being vivid orange with a black throat. They should be sown in a little heat in March or April and when large enough potted singly. They grow rapidly, soon reach flowering size, and may be either trained on the roof wires or round canes. They are sometimes kept pinched, that is, the young growth snipped out to keep them bushy, but it is doubtful if they will flower so freely when grown in this way. Closely allied is *T. gregorii* (syn. *T. gibsonii*) with bright orange flowers.

8 · Bulbs, Corms, and Tubers for Forcing

Bulbs for Forcing

When referring to bulbs one instinctively thinks of the period from Christmas to June. That is of course the time when bulbous plants are to be seen everywhere, but there are bulbous plants, using the term in the broad popular sense, which will flower right through the year.

It may be as well to explain this point. Botanically a bulb is defined as a modified shoot enveloped in scale leaves as in an onion, lily, or hyacinth. In the everyday usage of the bulb merchant and bulb catalogues the term 'dry bulb' is used to cover almost any storage organ whether bulb, corm, or rhizome, which can be kept for some time dormant, or almost dormant, and out of the soil. Most of them are from hot, dry regions of the earth, where they are naturally baked by the sun and thoroughly 'ripened'. This is a most important point in the cultivation of many bulbs. Nerines, for example, natives of South Africa, will not flower freely unless thoroughly ripened off in summer, preferably by a period on a sunny shelf or frame, and many others like a brief rest even though not completely dried off.

When good-quality bulbs are bought the flower is already present in embryo. All the gardener has to do for the first season in order to mature it, is to supply water and sufficient warmth and light. To carry the bulb on to subsequent years and flower it repeatedly does, however, require good cultivation. With such bulbs as tulips and hyacinths it is not worth trying, and even with daffodils it is best to plant out the bulbs for a year or two in the garden before forcing again.

Bulbs for early flowering are indispensable; practically all the spring-flowering ones may be used under glass if desired and few of them want or like hard forcing. It is of course possible to obtain prepared bulbs which will flower from Christmas onwards – hyacinths, for example, and the tazetta narcissus 'Paper White', 'Grand Monarque', and 'Soleil d'Or' which are naturally early. Scillas and chionodoxas also are early and require only a little protection to bring them along in February. From then on the greenhouse can be gay with freesias, lachenalias, narcissus, and tulips.

So far as forced bulbs are concerned the important point is that they must be potted early, not later than August. This gives them time to root freely before starting to force them about mid-November. For this purpose cold frames are excellent, but a sheltered situation out of doors will serve.

This does not of course imply that good-quality bulbs are not important. Size alone is no criterion when buying bulbs. That they should be firm and solid is of much greater importance.

Hyacinths

No flowers are more useful for very early greenhouse forcing than the hyacinth. The earliest are the prepared bulbs which have been subjected to treatment by the growers which makes them flower much earlier than the same varieties not so treated. If potted in August and brought into a warm house in November they should be in flower by Christmas. For later work, say from mid-January onwards, there are a number of suitable varieties in a wide range of colours; these are usually sold as top-size bulbs, second size being used for bedding and outdoor work. For even gentle forcing they should be in pots or bowls by early September and plunged under ashes until root growth is well advanced.

When taken out of the plunge bed the foliage will be white or yellow and they should be kept in shade, say under the stagings, until this is a normal green. Many growers keep them in shade for a time to draw up the foliage. It is never wise to mix varieties in one pot, as the flowering period varies. The number of bulbs per pot varies with the size of the bulbs; small single bulbs may be put in 3½-inch pots, large ones in 5-inch. Three of average size will usually go in a 6-inch. Keep half the bulb above the surface of the soil. It is an old but sound practice to place each bulb on a small mound of sand to check rot at the base of the bulb. They should then be plunged in ashes or sand to a depth of 2 to 4 inches over the bulbs and left for four or five weeks. After this period the early batches may, if frames are available, be moved into them. From this point on hyacinths are best under cover, as

75. Hyacinth. A good pan of the pale blue variety 'Perle Brillante'.

they should not be allowed to become too wet until growth is well advanced. When forced, small thin stakes or wires are advisable, as the flowers are heavy, and if the stems should collapse or bend it is difficult to make them look well again.

Varieties vary a good deal in forcing and it is better to use older and reliable ones rather than take chances with new and little-known ones. In white varieties I doubt if any is better than 'L'Innocence', in dark blues, 'Ostara', while 'Queen of the Blues' is a clear azure blue. 'Perle Brillante' (Plate 75) is also a good pale blue. In pink shades 'Lady Derby' is a salmon-pink and 'La Victoire' a darker rose-crimson. 'City of Haarlem' is un-usual, a creamy yellow.

All these can be obtained as prepared bulbs and may be brought into flower from Christmas onwards if potted early and gently forced. For later work a wider colour range is available; 'Orange Boven' ('Salmonette') is a lovely apricot-salmon, 'Princess Irene' a silvery pink, and one of the deepest colours is 'Tubergen's Scarlet'.

Narcissi

There can be few genera in which so much progress has been made in breeding in recent years as in this one. There is a wonderful range from which to choose. The genus is divided into nine main groups and in each group there are varieties suitable for cultivation in pots, in fact the greatest difficulty is in the selection.

For early forcing the bunch-flowered section or tazettas are very extensively used, the two best known being 'Paper White' and 'Soleil d'Or' (Plate 76), the latter being deep yellow with an orange cup. They are both naturally early, so do not require hard forcing. Amongst the newer varieties the best is probably 'Cragford' (Plate 77) which comes in about mid-January.

Those given are in the cheaper or moderate price range. There are also a number of varieties more recently raised which are rather higher in price but include some very fine ones.

The most popular group is still probably the large yellow trumpet type which are generally called daffodils. Of these, two old varieties still largely used are 'King Alfred' and 'Emperor'. Other varieties, raised slightly later and reasonably priced, are 'Godolphin', 'Unsurpassable', and 'Magnificence'. Of the trumpet varieties with white or primrose flowers I like 'Bonython' and 'Spring Glory', or if a pure white is wanted 'Beersheba' and the newer 'Mount Hood'.

It is when we come to the second group, those with the trumpet less than half the size of the perianth, that selection becomes difficult, as a great deal depends on individual opinion. Amongst the best of the cheaper bulbs with intense red cups and yellow perianths are 'Carbineer', 'Aranjuez', and 'Rustom Pasha'.

From those with white perianths and yellow or red cups, I would recommend 'Flower Record', one of the best for forcing, 'John Evelyn' with beautifully frilled margins, and for a larger

141

76. Narcissus 'Soleil d'Or' is an old variety but very popular for early
forcing.

77. Narcissus 'Cragford' is one of the best in its section and valuable for early flowering. White with an orange-scarlet crown.

and showy variety 'Marshal Tsjoekof'. 'Tunis' is also an easy and useful variety.

The next group are those with small cups, one of the best being 'La Riante' with a pure white perianth and red cup. 'Firetail' is a popular variety with creamy white perianth and crimson-scarlet cup. There are many very lovely varieties amongst the smaller species and varieties; I particularly like 'Thalia' with lovely white flowers carried two or three on a stem. The Jonquil group also are lovely in bowls or pots; my own favourite is 'Trevithian' which is also fragrant. A number of varieties can now be obtained which have been prepared or pre-cooled. These will flower a month or more earlier than naturally grown bulbs of the same varieties.

All varieties should be potted in August and September in J.I.P.$_1$ and immediately plunged in ashes for at least six weeks. If frame room is available they can then be moved into the frames, if not, some of the ashes should be taken off so that the foliage will not become too drawn. Successive batches can be started in the greenhouse from November to March, taking the earlier flowering varieties in first, and leaving those which do not force well, for example, the Poeticus, to the last. They will take plenty of water once they start into growth and most varieties will require staking or the foliage and possibly the flower stems may fall.

After flowering they should be gently hardened off (in a cold frame is best) and about the end of April they may be either naturalized in the garden or planted in nursery rows for a year or so, when they can again be used for pot cultivation.

It is not worth while keeping them in pots, as they will be so exhausted they would probably not flower the following year.

Tulips

Tulips are never better than when grown cold, and it follows that the less heat given the more normal will be colour and form.

For forcing early the best are the small single-flowered varieties. I find 'Brilliant Star' one of the most reliable of this group; it can be relied on from January onwards; another easy and reliable variety is 'Fred Moore' (Plate 78). I do not like the

78. Tulip 'Fred Moore'. One of the most reliable early varieties with terra-cotta, orange-tinged flowers.

double forms, but for those who do 'Peach Blossom' and 'Rhein-gold' are two good varieties, pink and yellow, as the names suggest.

The mendel type of tulip is also most useful for greenhouse work; they are early and single-flowered. For early work 'Pink Gem' and 'Piquante' are good, the latter being red; and 'Her Grace' is a useful white.

These early varieties must be potted in August and treated in the same manner as advised for hyacinths and narcissi. Later-flowering varieties, however, need not be potted until September or October and will come along naturally with very little heat.

Amongst the later-flowering groups are the lily-flowered which flower naturally in May; they are lovely under glass but do not require much heat. The Triumph group also are worth trying, they show the most amazing range of bicolors, stripes, and flushes in all shades. The Darwin group now has the most extensive range of self colours; all have long stems. Not all are suitable for forcing and at best they tend to become drawn and weak unless great care is taken. For use under glass the following are suitable. 'Aristocrat', purplish-violet; 'Niphetos', lemon-yellow; 'Princess Elizabeth', soft rose; 'Rose Copland', rich pink; and 'White Giant', a fine large white.

Lilies

There is no doubt that the true lilies are seen to best advantage in groups under natural conditions. Where such do not exist, however, as in a town garden, there is no reason why they should not be enjoyed in the greenhouse. Those which are easy to grow are just as easy in pots and those which are difficult in the garden are often easier to manage under glass. It is generally wise when potting to use the smallest pots which will hold them comfortably, usually one in a 7-inch pot or three in a 10-inch. This encourages free rooting and avoids overwatering. Several of the best species produce roots above the bulbs, and for this group a larger, deeper pot is used, at first only half filled. Later, when the stems are developing, 2 or 3 inches more compost is added so that the new roots can benefit from it.

With purchased bulbs the best advice is to pot at the earliest possible moment when received, first removing any dead or broken scales, and dusting with flowers of sulphur where damaged, to check further decay. It pays to go to a specialist firm or dealer in bulbs. The bulbs soon deteriorate and lose their vitality if exposed to the air. They should be stored in dry sand, soil, or fibre, while out of the ground, and those seen on shop counters, exposed to the air, are rarely worth buying.

The plants should at all times be kept cool, but are usually better in cold frames than plunged out of doors, as watering is easier to control. Once they are growing freely, watering may be more liberal, and when buds develop they may be given liquid manure or soot water. After flowering, they can be stood out of doors in a sheltered situation, though they must not be allowed to become too dry. They should be carried through the winter in protected frames or plunged in ashes. Early in the new year the drainage should be examined and an inch or two of good new compost be placed over the bulbs. But it is better to avoid touching the roots. One of the greatest enemies of lilies is the aphis, not only for the toll they can take from the plants themselves but also because they can transmit the deadly virus from plant to plant. An insecticide or fumigant should be used frequently to keep these under control.

If frame or nursery space is available lilies can readily be raised from seed, some species, e.g. *Lilium regale*, will often flower the second year. Apart from cost the main advantage is that you start with clean, healthy, and virus-free stock.

Without question the finest of the lilies is *Lilium auratum*, the golden-rayed lily of Japan (Plate 79). It is once again available from British-raised bulbs and, if obtained from a reliable source, will succeed well enough and give an immense amount of pleasure. It is less tolerant of lime than most species, so where J.I.P. soil is used the chalk is usually omitted, especially if the water is hard. There are many fine varieties. If unforced they do not flower until August or September. *L. brownii* has long funnel-shaped flowers, white within, brown without. It is some 3 to 4 feet in height and each stem will usually carry three or four flowers or more; it is July-flowering. Quite different, both in colour and habit, *L. davidii* is a slender graceful lily with orange-scarlet flowers borne

79. *Lilium auratum* 'Crimson Queen', one of the finest lilies for cultivation in pots.

in July and August. *L. × elegans* is available in a considerable range of varieties from lemon-yellow to crimson. These are dwarf compared to the others, being usually only 15 to 18 inches in height. *L. formosanum* is one of the loveliest of the white species, and one of the best for flowering under glass, especially as it is not very hardy. It is one of the quickest to flower from seed. If sown in autumn and kept growing, it will usually flower the following summer. *L. hansoni* is one of the Martagon groups of lilies, with golden flowers spotted with chocolate. It is vigorous and long-lived. *L. henryi* is a strong grower with rich orange flowers. Too tall perhaps for a small house, it may reach 8 feet in height. It is late, rarely flowering before August.

L. longiflorum, the white trumpet lily of the florists' shops, is perhaps best known as the Bermuda lily, though it originally came from the Ryuku Islands, south of Japan. It is probably the easiest lily to grow in pots but is not hardy enough to winter out of doors. This species is also easily raised from seed. Bulbs are usually available from about September, and it should be in

80. *Lilium speciosum* 'Melpomene', a lovely variety. It has crimson
    markings on a white ground.

flower about Easter. Bulbs are also imported from St Helena and become available about May; these, if handled at once, will bloom from September onwards, giving two flowering periods. These bulbs are not as a rule grown on, as the bulbs tend to break up and take some time to build up flowering size again.

L. × 'Marhan' is the result of crosses between the white form of *L. martagon* and *L. hansoni*. There are a number of named colour forms of varying shades of yellow and orange, spotted with reddish-brown and flowering in the open in June-July. *L.* × 'Princeps' is also of hybrid origin, but is too large for a small house. It is more or less intermediate between the parents, *L. sargentiae* and *L. regale*, and has white trumpet lilies, vigorous in growth, sometimes over 6 feet high, with twenty or more flowers. *L. regale* is well named Royal, though it is one of the easiest to grow and flower. It will carry up to fifteen flowers normally, with clear white trumpets on strong stems up to 6 feet in height. Out of doors it will flower in July. Seedlings will flower in their second year.

L. speciosum is, like *L. auratum*, of Japanese origin. It is one of the loveliest of pot plants and is autumn-flowering. In colour it ranges from pure white as in 'Album Novum', to rich red as in 'Melpomene' (Plate 80), with varying degrees of spotting and marking. *L. tigrinum* and its varieties are also amongst the easiest and best, but it does dislike lime. It is one of the easiest to perpetuate as it produces bulbils in the axils of the leaves. *L. willmottiae* is one of the most free-flowering of all lilies. It produces enormous spikes of orange-red, which require staking or they will fall with their own weight. It normally flowers in July and August.

There are many more which could be used under glass, but a line must be drawn somewhere. For most people, two or three are sufficient, but it is usually possible to establish them out of doors after flowering them in pots, and this gives an opportunity to try another species next year.

9 · Tender Bulbs, Corms, and Tubers

Everyone is familiar with the bulbous plants mentioned in the previous chapter as used under glass in winter and early spring. Very few gardeners, however, appreciate the wealth of bulbs, corms, and tubers which are available to the owner of a greenhouse and which with very little care and attention will flower year after year. South Africa in particular has provided a wealth of such material; for example, lachenalias, freesias, ixias, and tritonias.

All of these are easy to grow and require little heat, in fact our minimum of 45° F. will suffice. With this group it will probably be better to follow the calendar rather than alphabetical sequence.

Lachenalias are excellent for flowering from January onwards and last a long time in flower. The best known are the *L. aloides* group, known in gardens as *L. nelsonii* (Plate 81), the predominating colours being orange, yellow, and green. There are also purple and white species but they are little known in cultivation. They are potted in August, seven or eight bulbs to a 5-inch pot, and started into growth in a cold frame. After the first watering they are kept moderately dry until the foliage begins to develop, when watering must be gradually increased. When frost is imminent, say October, they should be taken into the house, preferably on a shelf near the glass to prevent the foliage becoming drawn. After flowering they are best returned to the greenhouse shelf to ripen and dry off the bulbs, and there they can remain until potting time in August, if space permits.

Freesias (Plate 82) are most valuable winter-flowering plants and once a stock is obtained they may be carried on from year to year. They should be obtained in August and potted in the usual way about five to seven corms in a 5-inch pot. They should be watered once to start them into growth, and placed in cold frames protected only from heavy rain, which might make them too wet before growth commences. Once they are

151

81. Lachenalias are easily grown bulbs for the cool greenhouse.

moving freely, however, they want plenty of water. As the foliage develops it is wise to give them a few twigs to climb through. The foliage hides this later and it is less unsightly and more natural than staking and tying, besides being somewhat less laborious.

When they finish flowering they can be returned to a protected frame, and should be kept growing vigorously and watered freely until about May when the foliage yellows and gradually dies off. The lights should be kept on from then onwards and the more thoroughly they are ripened the better. The dead foliage should be removed and a watch kept for mice, which enjoy them! In August they should be again shaken out of the pots and the largest corms repotted. If it is desired to build up stock of a good variety the small corms may also be grown on. These may not all flower the following year, but a fair proportion will and the rest will build up useful stock.

There is now a very lovely colour range available, clear lavenders, rich orange and yellow, and any number of bi-colors and diffused 'Rainbow' shades. Whites also are now strong and vigorous. They can also be easily raised from seed.

152

82. Freesias have been greatly improved in recent years, both in form and the range of colour.

83. Clivias. A fine group of hybrids.

Ixias and **Sparaxis.** Closely related botanically and requiring identical treatment are *Ixias* and *Sparaxis*, though they are later flowering. Amongst ixias are some of the most dazzling colours, including the most fascinating of green flowers, *I. viridiflora*. They are tall-growing and wiry with rush-like foliage. They should not be forced. From New Year onwards a sunny shelf suits them best and they flower in late spring or early summer. *Sparaxis* also provide brilliant colours, particularly orange and yellow. Another allied genus, *Babiana*, has curious flowers usually in blue, purple, and white.

They are all sun-lovers and not hardy enough for outdoor cultivation in most parts of Britain. They give a display over a period of several weeks in a sunny greenhouse.

Clivia also flower in spring and early summer. They are not true bulbs, but evergreens with thick, fleshy roots and leathery foliage. They are best grown in a greenhouse though in summer they will do in frames. They are vigorous growers and require large pots and liberal feeding while growing. There are many fine hybrids ranging in colour from yellow, through reds to maroon (Plate 83). The species, *C. miniata*, though smaller in flower, is wonderfully floriferous and not to be despised. After flowering they should be kept somewhat drier but never completely dried off.

84. *Hippeastrum rutilum* var. *fulgidum* comes from Tropical America. This is one of the species from which the cultivars have been developed and is smaller and more graceful in flower.

Hippeastrums (Plates 84 and 85), more generally called Amaryllis, have been greatly improved in recent years and there are now quite dwarf plants, obtainable in all shades of white, pink, red, and crimson. They should be started into growth from February onwards, preferably in succession. A fair-sized bulb will require a 6-inch pot and should be potted with most of the bulb above the surface and grown in a sunny place, or the foliage will become drawn and weak. They are usually dried off after the foliage dies down, but this can be overdone, and many growers keep them just moist.

Closely allied is the Jacobean lily, *Sprekelia formosissima*, with beautifully formed flowers of deep scarlet, and like velvet

155

85. Hippeastrums can be obtained in many shades of crimson and red, pink, and white.

86. *Vallota speciosa*, one of the most showy of bulbous plants and easily grown.

in texture. Another allied species which used to be a popular cottage window plant is *Vallota speciosa* (Plate 86). Though known as the Scarborough lily, it is in fact a native of South Africa. It is one of the easiest of bulbous plants to grow and flower and its brilliant red flowers are most striking. They should not be potted deeply and do not like too frequent disturbance or repotting. The mother bulb produces offsets on the surface which are easily detached and potted separately. Though they like sunshine and warmth they should never be completely dried off.

Amongst summer-flowering plants the blue-flowered *Agapanthus* have no rival. Like clivias they are perennials with fleshy root stocks rather than bulbs. They require plenty of water while growing, but are best rested almost dry and in a frost-free place for the winter. There are several nearly allied species and hybrids. Some of them can be grown out of doors in warm sheltered situations, but it is safer to winter them in the greenhouse and put them out of doors during the summer months. Cold and damp conditions in winter are usually fatal.

Begonias. The easiest and best for the cool house are the tuberous-rooted hybrid race (*B. tuberhybrida*). They provide a good range both in single and double flowers in all shades of red, pink, yellow, and of course white (Plate 87). For a start it is usually best to buy a few dry tubers in the same way as bulbs; named varieties are of course expensive, but unnamed tubers obtained from specialist growers are sure to contain good forms, and from the best of these seed can be saved and the next generation can be your own raising. Under cool conditions it is not wise to start them into growth too early; March is early enough. They should then be placed *rounded side down, hollow side up*, and left until roots are developed. They can either be started in boxes or laid out on the border, but they should be in light leafy soil, and above all well-drained. When well rooted they can be potted off singly according to the size of the tuber, usually a $3\frac{1}{2}$-inch pot is large enough to start with. Keep the atmosphere moist but water sparingly and carefully at first, and shade the plants when the sun becomes strong.

After flowering, watering should be gradually reduced, and

87. Begonias. A nice group of double tuberous-rooted varieties.

as the foliage dies away the pots should be laid on their sides under the staging. During the winter they can be shaken out of the pots and cleaned ready to start the whole cycle over again.

Haemanthus, the Blood Flowers, are of two different groups, one requires thorough drying off, the other does not.

The red-flowered *H. coccineus* has bold deep green foliage in the summer months, goes to rest in late summer, and flowers in spring before the new foliage appears. The smaller white-flowered *H. albiflos* (Plate 88) flowers in autumn. *H. multiflorus* and *H. katherinae* (Plate 89) never completely go to rest though the old foliage dies off in winter and new growth starts almost immediately. These two are summer-flowering and have huge orange-scarlet inflorescences. All of these will go several years without repotting, though the two last-named do tend to climb out of their pots. They are rather too large for small houses.

Tigridia pavonia can now be obtained in an extensive colour range. They are striking (Plate 90) but unfortunately short-lived flowers. For cultivation in pots the bulbs should be

88. *Haemanthus albiflos* can be grown in the same pot for several years. It is never more than a foot or so in height.

89. *Haemanthus katherinae* is much larger and much more leafy. It is most striking in flower.

159

90. *Tigridias* are most brilliant in colour. They are extremely easy to grow.

potted in autumn, three or four to a 5-inch pot, and plunged in ashes in cold frames. Watering may be begun as foliage is developed and they must be either brought into the greenhouse or thoroughly protected from frost during winter. They require similar treatment to gladioli.

Watsonia. Closely related to gladioli, these plants require winter protection; for pot culture they are potted between October and March and grown in a protected cold frame or cool house. They flower in late summer. The best known is the white-flowered *W. ardernei* but the brick-red *W. fulgens* is also good.

91. *Hedychium coronarium* is one of the smallest species and very
fragrant.

Hedychiums and **Cannas** are perennial herbs grown from fleshy
rhizomes which are divided and potted early in the new year
to flower during the summer months.

The best-known and hardiest of the Hedychiums is *H.*
gardnerianum, though it is too vigorous for small houses.
H. coronarium (Plate 91) is one of the most sweetly and powerfully scented flowers, with pure white flowers and not more
than 3 or 4 feet in height. Cannas are excellent for greenhouse
cultivation. The foliage is handsome and the flowers are

161

amongst the most brilliant of tropical herbs. The rhizomes are overwintered in a dry state usually ready to start into growth in February or March. The old rhizomes should be knocked out of the pots and divided either into single crowns for 6- or 7-inch pots or larger pieces if 9-inch pots are to be used. A temperature of 50° F. is quite enough to start them into growth and watering should be done sparingly until they are growing freely, after which it can be liberal. Good varieties are 'President' and 'Louis Cayeux' (both red), 'King Humbert' (orange), 'R. Wallace' (yellow), and 'Tyrol' (pink). After flowering, watering can be gradually reduced till the foliage dies off and the plants placed under the benches to ripen off.

Achimenes. There are a number of species and hybrids in a good range of colour. They are excellent for pot work if staked and equally good for hanging baskets in which they are allowed to hang naturally. Where plenty of heat is available they can be potted from the end of January to flower about mid-June, but in the cool house April or May is early enough and they will then flower in late summer and autumn. The tubers are usually boxed in a light sandy compost until growth starts, and then potted into 5- or 7-inch pots or baskets. While growing they like atmospheric humidity and should be kept as close to the glass as possible to keep them 'stocky'; shade will be necessary during sunny weather. After flowering, water should be gradually reduced and when the foliage becomes yellow the pots should be turned on their sides under the bench to rest the tubers. The easiest method of propagation is by division of the tubers when potting. Seeds, if obtained, usually germinate freely, but the hybrids will probably not come true.

Polianthes tuberosa. The tuberose is not often seen nowadays, but it is one of the most powerfully scented flowers and extremely popular in warmer countries. One of the daffodil family, it is a native of Mexico. The bulbs are usually bought, flowered, and discarded, as they exhaust themselves in flowering and it takes some time to build them up to flowering size again in this country. Water sparingly until they are growing freely, then liberally. 'The Pearl' is the best variety – a good double and not too tall.

Zephyranthes candida is a white-flowering species from the River Plate, the flowers are rather like a crocus but are borne on long peduncles like daffodils. They are seen to best advantage if grown several bulbs in a large pan. They are hardy in the south and for pot cultivation can be treated as near-hardy and grown in protected cold frames, being stood out of doors in summer until the flowering season about August. A number of species formerly grown as *Zephyranthes* are now known as *Habranthus*.

Nerine. These are one of the most valuable of autumn-flowering bulbs and possess a wonderful range of colour, from white through all shades of pink (Plate 92) and salmon to deepest scarlet and in recent years even purple. They are not the easiest of bulbs and when potted will frequently refuse to flower until thoroughly re-established. For that reason never disturb them while they are doing well. If they are really starving, move the clump on without breaking it up. Flowers are produced before the leaves, or just as they begin to develop, and they should be given plenty of water from then onwards until May or June when the foliage dies off. The bulbs then require a rest and the most thorough baking you can give them; the best place for them is a sunny shelf near the glass. They are natives of South Africa and such sun as we have in this country is not going to hurt them. By the way, the bulbs should not be buried in potting but left half above soil level as in planting hyacinths or shallots!

Amaryllis belladonna can usually be grown and flowered successfully at the base of a south wall. Where such facilities do not exist they provide easy and beautiful autumn-flowering bulbs for the cool house. They will do well in cold frames and can be brought into the greenhouse for flowering from September onwards. This is quite distinct from the 'Amaryllis' of the nurseryman (Hippeastrum).

Zantedeschia aethiopica, or Richardia, the Calla or Arum lily, is naturally a moisture-loving plant and requires plenty of water while growing, and rich feeding. It will flower under glass from September onwards through the winter. About April the plants can be hardened off in the shelter of a hedge or similar situation, and a month or so later they should be planted out in the kitchen garden or nursery border until September.

92. Nerine. An unusually fine pale pink hybrid. They are most valuable
for autumn colour.

They are far happier and healthier treated in this way than
when kept in pots. In September lift and pot up the best tubers,
not more than three to a 10-inch pot, and place in a protected
frame until new growth makes it necessary to bring into the
greenhouse.

The lovely yellow *Z. elliottiana* is more tender and it is better
to dry off and rest for a while, keeping it under glass. Equally
tender are *Z. pentlandii*, deep yellow with a black basal blotch,
and *Z. rehmannii* in varying shades of pink to violet.

10 · Forcing Hardy Plants

Some of our loveliest spring-flowering shrubs (and if head room permits small trees) can make an excellent display if brought on gently under glass. They will never repay their keep if neglected, but well cared for they can be delightful in the early months of the year.

To be successful with flowering shrubs it is necessary to have them well established in the pots. They should be plunged in a bed in a sunny situation and well watered and fed to build up the flower buds. Established plants can be kept in good health for many years by judicious pruning after flowering and liberal feeding afterwards. The first batch can usually be brought into the house after the chrysanthemums are cleared. As these come into flower, others should be brought in to succeed them as required.

The number of plants which can be forced in this way is limited by the fact that in a small house it is difficult to know how to deal with those which have passed out of flower. It is too early in the year to risk them out of doors in a soft condition, and the best compromise is to prune them back and place them in the least conspicuous place in the house until such time as one can risk standing them out in a sheltered situation. This difficulty is sometimes got over in spring by covering plants which have been forced with tiffany to check frost damage, and gradually hardening off.

When buying shrubs for forcing, tell the nurseryman you want them for this purpose and he will select well-budded plants suitable for flowering the first season. They should be obtained as early as possible after leaf fall.

Dead twigs, pruning snags, and any twiggy useless wood should be first cut away, and also any broken or damaged roots. They should then be potted firmly into the smallest size possible without damaging the roots. Plants lifted in this way usually require large pots. Give good drainage, pot firmly, and then plunge. For this purpose weathered ashes or sand are best, but if not available a garden border will serve. In December those wanted early can

93. *Chaenomeles
lagenaria*, the
Japanese
Quince.

be brought into the greenhouse, little watering will be needed at first, but after a week or two, as they dry out, watering should be increased. They should be frequently syringed to soften the buds, but not when the buds begin to show colour.

Forsythia. One of the easiest and most widely used shrubs for this purpose is *Forsythia*, particularly the variety *F. intermedia spectabilis*. Prepared plants need not be brought into heat until December or January and will be in flower in a week or two. There are several newer varieties which should widen the range of colour. One is called 'Nymans' variety and another 'Lynwood' variety, while for a very small house I should suggest *F. ovata* and a recently introduced American variety, *F.* 'Bronxensis', the latter being the dwarf of the family.

There are some first-class shrubs for forcing in the Rose family. One of the earliest and best is the cottage gardener's 'Japonica', *Chaenomeles lagenaria* (Plate 93), in white, pink, and vermilion.

94. *Prunus triloba.*
The photograph
shows it as a
wall shrub, but
it is equally
good for gentle
forcing.

Prunus. For small houses two Prunus are lovely: *P. japonica* in
pink and white and *P.* (or Amygdalus) *tenella.* After flowering,
these, unlike the cherries to which they are related, can be
pruned right back to the base of the shoots. They will make new
shoots a foot or so long and carry next season's flowers, so that
they need never be taller than 2 feet 6 inches to 3 feet. *P. triloba*
also can be hard pruned in much the same way (Plate 94).

Where the gardener has plenty of head room and facilities
for 'hardening off' after flowering there are many species and
varieties at his disposal. Peaches are excellent, both double-
flowered and single; good doubles are *P. persica* 'Aurora'
(Plate 95) and 'Iceberg'. The almond is even earlier and is
easily brought into flower, and closely related is *P. davidiana*
in pink and white, and the hybrid *P.* 'Accolade' (Plate 96). All
the cherries are beautiful, though they tend to become too
large for a small house.

Other shrubs which can be kept small are *Deutzia gracilis,*

95. *Prunus persica*
'Aurora'.

with lovely white flowers, and *Spiraea thunbergii*, also white. *Spiraea arguta* is equally lovely but somewhat larger.

Lilacs also are lovely and can be obtained in an extensive colour range, though colours are never so vivid under glass as in the open. The old *Kerria japonica* variety *plena* can be effective, and also the smaller single flowered species. The hybrid *Cytisus* or brooms are useful for later use, from about April onwards. Laburnums are most graceful for indoor flowering, as is also wistaria.

In selecting shrubs for forcing always try to keep a balance in colour (yellow, for example, with plants such as forsythia, kerria, and laburnum can easily be overdone, and so of course can pink and white unless care is taken), as there are so many from which to select. To avoid this make a point of using lilac, and if room allows, wistaria. Pot-grown roses are also excellent for late spring and early summer; selection is largely a matter of personal choice, but it is always wise to find out from the grower whether a particular favourite will force

96. Prunus 'Accolade' is one of the best of the hybrid cherries.

satisfactorily. Growing roses under glass is described in Chapter 9 of F. Fairbrother's book in this series, *Roses*.

Herbaceous Plants

Many of these are useful for forcing purposes. Most of the hardy *Astilbes* will flower in the greenhouse during the early spring months; they are available in a good range of shades from white to deep red and maroon. The best white is probably 'Prof. van der Weilen'; 'Rhineland' and 'Ceres' are pink, and 'Granat' and 'Gertrude Brix' crimson.

97. *Dicentra spectabilis*, a delightful plant for late winter and early spring.

Dicentra spectabilis (Bleeding Heart or Dutchman's Breeches) (Plate 97) is another good plant for the purpose. With very gentle forcing it will flower from February onwards. Plants should be lifted and potted in autumn and wintered in a cold frame. After flowering they should be gradually hardened off and may then be replanted in the garden.

Several of the hardy primulas can be used in the same way, though only for the one season. A good strain of polyanthus or coloured primrose will provide plenty of colour if potted in autumn, kept in frost-free frames until January, and then gently forced. Several of the candelabra group are equally good, particularly *Primula pulverulenta* in variety. *P. denticulata* is also good.

11 · Orchids

Not so very many years ago British gardens were famous for their collections of orchids. The species were imported in quantity from Central and South America and from India and the Far East and sold by auction in London. Two disastrous wars have put an end to many large private collections. There are, however, indications that small collections of hybrids, particularly of cool house orchids, are now coming back into favour. By the use of up-to-date houses with thermostatic control of heating and ventilation much of the day-to-day routine is eliminated and the modern gardener can find time enough to cope with his plants.

While it is true that cool house orchids require somewhat different conditions from the majority of cool house plants they are no more difficult to manage. *Cymbidiums* and some species of *Cypripedium* and *Coelogyne* can in fact be grown as part of a mixed collection.

These will all thrive with our minimum of 45° F. Where they differ from the more ordinary greenhouse plant is that they prefer a higher degree of humidity and more shade during hot weather. It must be remembered that they are natives of humid forests, where they actually grow as epiphytes attached to the trunks and limbs of trees.

It is for this reason that they are usually grown in specially well-drained, yet moisture-retaining, composts. They may be grown in pots, pans, or other receptacles such as wooden rafts and baskets. The latter are of course more suitable for suspension from wires, but the pots and pans are usually stood on inverted pots a foot or so above the stage or bench. The bench itself and floor underneath is covered with coke breeze, coarse ashes, or shingle, with the object of holding as much moisture as possible, and so spaced as to allow syringing or damping between pots without unduly saturating the compost. The benches must obviously be strongly built, and rustless materials are best. Concrete benches, though they may look merely utilitarian, are extremely good and hygienic.

Before starting there are two steps which the novice should take, both of which may save him a good deal both in pocket and time and trouble. The first is to get into touch with a good orchid nursery and learn how they are grown by the nurseryman, and, secondly, to become a member of the thriving young Amateur Orchid Growers' Society. This will enable him to exchange ideas, see and handle all kinds of plants, and hear talks by experts on the genera he intends to grow.

There are several good books available, but to my mind a must for a beginner is *Orchids and their Cultivation* by David Sander and Edward Cooper, two names which are familiar to all the older generation of growers. At an orchid nursery he will obtain a better idea of the conditions required and how to maintain them than from either the written or spoken word. The nurseryman is always ready to advise and is usually more concerned with keeping a potential customer and getting him started, than with quick sales. He will also be able to advise what kinds and varieties or hybrids will be most suitable for the beginner's own conditions.

For orchids an entirely different range of potting materials is necessary. For most of them the basis is fibre, either osmunda fibre or polypodium fibre, which are actually the dead stems of the ferns of those two genera cleaned and pulled to pieces or chopped up. With this is incorporated charcoal and sphagnum moss, the former to keep the compost aerated and sweet, and the latter to hold the moisture. Sometimes coarse peat and dry bracken stems are also used.

With orchid composts there is a good deal more latitude in the proportions used, and opinions differ widely. For plants which, like cymbidiums, have pseudo-bulbs or water-storage organs, a lighter, more porous compost is used. Suitable compost may be obtained ready prepared from the principal sundriesmen, but always say for what genus or group you need it. For those who prefer to make their own I would recommend two parts each osmunda fibre and the fibre from peat or loam to one of sphagnum moss and one of drainage material such as washed broken pots and charcoal.

It will be noticed that there are two main groups of orchids,

98. *Cypripedium insigne*, one of the original species from which the modern hybrids have been derived, but still a good plant for a cool greenhouse.

one with swollen stems or water-storage organs known as pseudo-bulbs, and the other without. For this latter group, mainly cypripediums, a little heavier compost is used.

This contains more loam fibre; that is, turf from which all the fine particles have been shaken out and is used at 3 parts loam fibre, 1 part fibre or fibrous peat, 1 part sphagnum. Some growers add charcoal and crock and others use, instead of loam fibre, a by-product of the tanneries, tan bark.

The technique of potting is also somewhat different with these materials. The pot is filled one-third full of crocks, many growers placing them vertically to obtain better drainage. Next, the young lead is placed in the centre of the new pot and the materials worked in amongst its roots and round the collar with a potting stick or rammer until the plant is held firmly in place. In cypripedium it is often better to put several leads in a pot, three to a 5-inch or more in a larger size. In this case each lead is first balled in a little compost so that when placed in position they are kept an inch or two apart and the growths are faced outwards. The old pseudo-bulbs are cut away leaving only young and vigorous ones in the new pot, but the old ones need not be discarded. If placed in sphagnum and kept in a closed case they will usually

173

send out new shoots from the 'eyes' at the base of the pseudo-bulb. This is in fact the customary method of vegetative propagation of orchids, in addition to division.

The time of potting varies with the genus but the best moment is when new growth and roots appear from the base of the pseudo-bulbs. It should only be done if they are growing over and away from the old pot or, alternatively, if the compost has become sour.

They should go two or three years without completely re-potting, but a little surface dressing and new sphagnum worked into the surface is usually given as an annual overhaul. After potting less water is given, but to compensate, a higher humidity should be maintained for a week or two until the plants are growing freely.

A new technique in watering has to be learned as the tests for a normal compost do not apply with fibre. The plants should be kept just moist, but never sodden, throughout the growing season, and of course drier during the winter. Overwatering is an all too frequent cause of casualties.

Usually it is the best plan to examine all the orchids once a week in winter and twice weekly in spring, summer, and early autumn. Judge the weight of the plant; if it feels heavy leave it till next time, if 'light', then give a soaking. Observation and practice will soon give confidence. Plants with no pseudo-bulbs do naturally require careful watching, for they must not dry out completely.

While draughts should be avoided, ventilation is essential, particularly from April to September, and temperatures should not be allowed to become too high. Box ventilators and ridge ventilation will usually provide sufficient circulation, but if side ventilation is also available make sure that it is always on the leeward side.

Should it be possible to keep a winter minimum temperature of, say, 55° F., all the vast range of intermediate orchids become possible. Some of the lovely hybrid cattleyas and laelio-cattleyas would be worth trying. Laelias, miltonias, oncidiums, dendrobiums, and many others could be tried with every prospect of success. If they did nothing else, wartime conditions and restrictions proved that most orchids, if kept on the dry side, stand a good deal lower temperatures than were thought necessary.

The raising of orchids from seed is a fascinating business but a slow and difficult process. It is best left to the orchid grower or the experienced amateur grower.

One advantage of cool house orchids is that many of these flower during the winter months. Cymbidiums and cypripediums are especially valuable and even with hybrid odontoglossums and odontiodas there is often an odd 'scape' in winter; all these flowers are long-lasting. Another advantage to keep in mind is that the main potting dates for these plants are early spring when working conditions are usually not so good out of doors.

Given a small greenhouse with plenty of ventilation the beginner could not do better than start with a few seedling cymbidiums. If he has patience and is prepared to wait a year or two for his flowers, small unnamed seedlings are obtainable for a few shillings each and the parentage is usually supplied with the plants. They must be regarded as a gamble in that the seedlings may be quite different from the parents, but at the same time bear in mind that there is always the chance of a winner turning up and the plant being worth much more than you paid for it.

Modern hybrid cymbidiums (Plate 99) are vigorous in habit, free-flowering, and are lovely in both colour and texture. They are also one of the longest lasting flowers. On the plant they will remain a month in good condition, and even when cut last a surprisingly long time.

During the growing months April to September they will require frequent watering, possibly once or twice per week, but do not think that because they like humidity they are bog plants and should be kept soaked. During the winter they can be kept relatively dry and their pseudo-bulbs will carry them quite a long time without injury. Wherever possible use rain-water in preference to tap-water; this will also help to keep the sphagnum moss used in the compost alive and in good condition. In the genus *Cypripedium* (Plate 100) the Himalayan *C. insigne* (Plate 98) is the most reliable and best suited to the cool house. There are a number of varieties and an even greater range of hybrids, most of which are winter-flowering. The group of cypripedium with

99. *Cymbidium*, a fine modern variety.

100. *Cypripedium*, an up-to-date variety showing the rounded shape of flower.

mottled or tessellated foliage is much less hardy and should not be attempted at first. Repotting is only necessary when they become overcrowded or, as often happens, the compost begins to break up and disintegrate. It is then advisable to shake them right out and divide into small pieces. After potting keep the atmosphere rather more humid and the plants just moist and shaded.

With *Coelogyne*, by far the best species for the beginner is *C. cristata* and its varieties. Rather straggling in habit, it should be grown in large shallow pans and the growths pegged down to keep them within reasonable bounds. These are also winter-flowering. Another good genus for the cool house is *Odontoglossum*, which has a wonderful range of form and colour. Undoubtedly it is more difficult and the others should be tried first.

Dendrobium nobile is also an excellent plant. It flowers in March or April. The flowers are white tinged with rose with a deep purple throat. It has long, slender pseudo-bulbs which take little space. They are often grown suspended from wires from the roof and seem to thrive in this way as they receive plenty of light.

Though in favoured localities the lovely plants *Pleiones* may be grown in the Alpine House or even out of doors, most gardeners prefer to treat them as cool house orchids. There are several species, the best known and probably the most beautiful being *P. pricei* and *P. formosana* (Plate 102). The two species are much alike and have in fact been regarded as forms of one species by some authorities. Both are spring-flowering, each pseudo-bulb usually producing one flower. The perianth segments are purplish, the lip is paler suffused with brown and with yellow lines. They are deciduous, the foliage dying away in autumn, leaving plump little pseudo-bulbs sitting on the compost. The orchid grower is not unduly worried by pests and diseases. Thrips and red spider will flourish under hot, dry conditions and the liberal use of the syringe is the best preventive. There are specially made smokes designed to control both these pests, B.H.C. for thrips and Azobenzine for red spider. Tiny slugs can do damage to young roots out of all proportion to their size and should be watched for. The most effective remedy is liquid Slugit, applied with a fine rose to stages and moisture-holding materials.

101. *Odontoglossum*, a fine variety derived from *O. crispum*.

102. *Pleione formosana*.

12 · Pelargoniums

The 'Geranium' or, as it should be called, *Pelargonium*, provides excellent material for the amateur who has a greenhouse with just sufficient heat to exclude frost. Their cultivation and propagation is the easiest, and material can be raised for the house, garden, and greenhouse. Plants rooted from cuttings will make good flowering plants within six months of insertion. Cuttings should not be too soft and sappy – they are best taken from plants which have been kept dry and the cut surface allowed to dry before inserting. They will take no harm from such treatment, and it goes far in avoiding rotting after insertion. The cutting pots should be sunk to the rim in soil, sand, or ashes. This is usually done in frames, but rooting can be done in the open in August and September. The cuttings must be potted and protected in any case before the nights become too cold, and through the winter little water will be necessary. In March they can go into 5-inch pots and be gradually hardened off if they are to be planted out. If for flowering under glass, they will benefit from liquid feeding from April onwards, and the closer they are grown to the glass, the more compact will be the ultimate plant. In order to keep them short and stocky the leading shoot is pinched out, but this should not be done after February for flowering in May. These early-flowering plants can be cut back in July, rested for a time, and again potted on for autumn flowering. Cuttings rooted in spring may also be disbudded in the summer and used for autumn flowering.

'Geranium' means to most people what the botanist calls *Pelargonium*. The use of both names would not matter a great deal if we did not have the hardy species of true *Geranium* in our gardens. All true geraniums are natives of the northern temperate regions, whereas pelargoniums are from sub-tropical regions, chiefly South Africa, and are not of course hardy in Britain. The cultivated varieties so widely used for bedding purposes in parks and gardens, botanically *P. hortorum*, are known as zonal pelargoniums, because most of them have markings or zones of different colour in the leaves. This feature is inherited from the wild species from which they have been developed; chiefly, I believe, *P. zonale* and *P. inquinans*.

There is a considerable number of varieties from which to select (more correctly known as cultivars) and a very wide range of colour. Too often one is limited by the few varieties grown by the florist for 'bedding' purposes – usually the ubiquitous scarlet 'Paul Crampel', the vermilion 'Gustav Emich', the more or less orange 'Maxim Kovaleski', and the semi-double pink 'King of Denmark'. There are now several nurseries which specialize in the family and offer an extensive range of varieties. The young but flourishing Geranium Society is also publishing a quarterly bulletin, giving advice on the cultivation and selection of varieties. There are also several popular books dealing with the family, so there is no lack of information available. The number of varieties is too great for me to give much of a selection, and colours are very much a matter of individual taste.

For growing under glass the very large flowers are useful. 'Dagata', for instance, is a first-class show plant with magenta semi-double flowers. There are few better doubles than 'Decorator'. I think this is identical with 'President Baillet', and is also listed as 'Red Denmark'. It is soft red-scarlet in colour.

Among the purples there can be few better than 'Festiva maxima' syn. 'A. M. Mayne', but this is a difficult colour to stage, as it does not mix well. The double vermilion 'Gustav Emich' is becoming almost as well-known in London as the London Plane. Not only is it used in quantity round Buckingham Palace, but it is extensively planted to brighten up the parks and gardens all over the city. For a double white I should select 'Hermine'. A good single white is 'Cresta', and for a single pink I like 'Salmon Paul Crampel'.

A recently introduced variety of outstanding merit is 'Elisabeth Cartwright' – carmine with a distinct 'eye' (Plate 103). It was given the Award of Merit of The Royal Horticultural Society in 1950, and a rarer award, the Sander Medal for the best new greenhouse plant shown during the year, in 1951. Another Award of Merit was won in 1953 by a white variety, 'Edward Humphris'. It is from the same raiser and bears his own name.

103. Pelargonium 'Elizabeth Cartwright'.

For those who find variegated and coloured leaves fascinating there are varieties with varying degrees of silver and gold or purple and bronze foliage, and some of the tricolours, once so widely appreciated, are again available. The latter group were once so highly regarded that the flowers were removed in order to emphasize the rich colouring of the foliage.

In the silver-leaved group I still like 'Flower of Spring', largely because the flower colour is a clear vermilion without the hint of magenta which spoils some of the others. 'Caroline Schmidt' is a vigorous variety with bold double flowers which contrast with the white variegation of the foliage. 'Chelsea Gem' syn. 'Mrs Churchill' is a similar green, with a white margin and double rather washy pink flowers. For edging purposes either under glass or out of doors the old dwarf-growing 'Mme

104. Pelargonium 'Mrs Henry Cox', often grown for its distinctive
coloured leaves.

Salleron' is still a favourite, and as it rarely flowers no disbudding
is required. There is a sport from it called 'Little Trot', which
does flower. A good trio of gold-leaved varieties are 'Golden
Harry Hieover', 'Mrs Quilter', and 'Maréchal McMahon'. The
two last-named are almost identical except in flower colour. The
yellow-leaved variety 'Verona' is also useful for contrast. All
these varieties are old, probably very old, but they are still among
the best. In the tricolour group also, two of the old varieties,
'Mrs Henry Cox' (Plate 104), with bronze-red and creamy yellow
variegation, and 'Miss Burdett Coutts', variegated green and red
on yellow or ivory ground, are excellent. Another valuable old
stager is 'Mrs Pollock', also yellow margined with a zone of
brown, green, and purple in varying degrees, and a green centre.
The flowers are single, and scarlet. 'Happy Thought', though not

183

a tricolour, is interesting in that the colours are reversed. It is a green leaf with a creamy white centre, and single cherry-red flowers.

For the benefit of those interested in plant curiosities, I would recommend the plant variously known as 'Skelly's Pride' (Plate 105) and 'Salmon Fringed' (or 'Flame'). It is what is known as a chimera, and produces two varieties from one plant, the former a salmon-pink single flower with rounded petals and normal hairy foliage, while the name 'Salmon Fringed' accurately describes the flower of the other, and its foliage is hairless and shiny. Another similar plant is called 'Double New Life'. This produces double scarlet and white flowers and occasionally normal single scarlet flowers.

Some of these varieties, particularly the tricolour group, are more difficult to root. Cuttings should be taken in August and they should be rooted straight into 60-size pots so that no move is required before spring. I also find it quite worth while to use J.I.P. compost for these cuttings.

The ivy-leaved pelargoniums are supposed to be mainly descended from *P. peltatum*, but there is little doubt that they are of hybrid origin. They were formerly grown in tremendous quantity and a fair range of variety for window boxes and baskets. There are several varieties from which to select. The best-known is probably 'Madame Crousse', with pink flowers. 'Souvenir de Chas. Turner' is rose madder in colour and there are two or three with mauve to violet flowers, of which 'Abel Carrière' and 'Blue Peter' are amongst the best. An old variegated-leaved variety now popular as a house plant is 'L'Élégante' (Plate 106). Well named, this is pleasing in its fresh young foliage and even better in autumn when this assumes a violet colour. The flowers are bluish-pink.

The plants generally known in this country as Regal pelargoniums, botanically *P. domesticum*, have been somewhat out of favour in recent years but are quite definitely making a 'comeback'. They are somewhat more tender and have the disadvantage of a shorter flowering season, but they contain such a wonderful range of colours, blends, and contrasts that no collection of pelargoniums would be complete without some of them. I

105. Pelargonium
'Skelly's Pride'.

106. Pelargonium
'L'Élégante', an
unusually fine
pot. This variety
is often grown for
the colour of its
leaves.

107. Pelargonium 'Grand Slam'.

personally like 'Kantara', white with amethyst blotches, 'Rosy
Morn', rose-pink and amaranth, and 'Ruby', which is also well-
named. Many people are fascinated by the almost black varieties,
such as 'Lord Bute', velvety purple with carmine margin, and
'Black Knight', with a white margin. At the trial of 'Regals' at
Wisley in 1952 'Carisbrooke' was given an Award of Merit, and
in 1957 a First Class Certificate. It has large frilled flowers, rose-
coloured with a deep maroon blotch. Three varieties were Highly
Commended – 'Helen Ludgate', 'Melbourne', and 'Bath's
Carnival'. An Award of Merit was given in 1956 to a very fine
American-raised variety called 'Grand Slam' (Plate 107). It is
geranium lake in colour with deep purple markings.

108. *Pelargonium tomentosum.*

Many people are fond of the species and scented-leaved varieties, and classes are provided at the Geranium Society's show for them. They are certainly diverse and interesting, but naturally do not give the same return, from a decorative point of view, as the zonal cultivars. They are no more difficult to grow, but must have plenty of light and air at all times, be thoroughly ripened in autumn, and kept on the dry side during the winter. Amongst the best are *P. crispum* and its variegated variety, *P. tomentosum* (Plate 108), with large green, strongly peppermint-scented leaves, and the small-leaved, silvery-grey, and scented *P. fragrans.*

13 · Chrysanthemums

The 'Golden Flowers' are certainly amongst the oldest of garden flowers. They were said to have been cultivated in China 2000 years ago and in Japan as early as A.D. 386.

There is reason to think that they were first introduced to England about 1754 from China and one variety was cultivated by Phillip Miller in the Apothecaries' Garden at Chelsea in 1764. This stock was apparently lost, and a new stock was obtained from France in 1789. We know that by 1826 no less than forty-eight varieties were growing in the Horticultural Society's Gardens at Chiswick. Probably most of these were of Chinese origin, for we know that the East India Tea Company were bringing them over. An interesting date is 1830, for then we are told seedlings were being raised, particularly in France.

There is little doubt that 'Chrysanths' or 'Mums' are the most popular of all the specialist flowers. Above all, they have the advantages that they are almost hardy, and in consequence they leave the greenhouse free all summer for other purposes. Different methods of cultivation are favoured, often depending on climatic and other local conditions, but without question the best grown plants are those which are entirely grown in pots.

The great advantage is that unlike those which are lifted and potted or replanted in inside borders they do not suffer any check, and it is slow and regular growth which builds up blooms of show standards. This applies particularly to the late-flowering varieties; for October and early November varieties which are in bud when 'lifted in' the check is not so serious.

No genus, except perhaps auricula, has had so many and such varied composts recommended. Most head gardeners of the old school had their own private and secret formula. Today most growers find that the John Innes composts properly made give excellent results. The usual sequence is: cuttings in J.I. cutting compost; first potting in $J.I._1$; next move $J.I._2$ (i.e. a double dose of J.I. base and chalk); and final potting in $J.I._3$.

An important point in successful cultivation is the care of the

1. Cuttings of chrysanthemum. From left to right, large, medium, and small cuttings prepared for rooting. The ideal cutting is on the right. *By permission of Mr J. B. Stevenson.*

old plant or 'stools' after flowering, and the selection of cuttings. Thin spindly cuttings, hard and woody material, and too vigorous and sappy cuttings should all be rejected where possible. With certain 'cutting shy' varieties one cannot always be too particular. Those known to be shy in producing young shoots should be shaken out and repotted after flowering and given a little more warmth and care.

The time-honoured method is to take the cutting when 2 to 3 inches long, cut all but two pairs of leaves off and insert in the prepared cutting compost. This procedure is, by some propagators, condemned on the grounds that the use of the knife may transmit virus. They simply break off the cutting and insert without even trimming.

Where only a small number of plants are being grown the cuttings may be inserted singly into 3-inch pots, but the more usual practice is either to place five or six round the rim of a 3-inch pot or to line them out in boxes about 1½ inches apart. Where a quantity are being grown they are lined out in a propagating case or frame.

Some varieties suitable for use in small pots may be rooted in March or even later. These are kept pinched back at every second leaf so that bushy little plants are produced to flower in 6- or 7-inch pots. The pom-pom group and some of the singles are best for this purpose. The rooting of cuttings and subsequent cultivation differs little from the general run of greenhouse plants. The important thing is that the late-flowering varieties

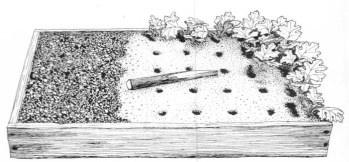

2. A cutting box (2 by 9 by 14 inches) showing the soil with a layer of sand on top; the dibber with which the cuttings are inserted; the spacing of the cuttings; and a few cuttings in place. *By permission of Mr J. B. Stevenson.*

should be rooted early and given the longest possible time to build up. For show purposes many growers start with cuttings in December and try to have the young plants established in 3-inch pots before the end of February.

They should be potted into J.I.$_1$ potting compost, not too firmly potted, and above all grown on in the lightest possible situation to prevent them becoming drawn and weak. At this

3. A really good box of cuttings which should be in the coolest place possible – there should be no delay in giving them their next move into beds of soil or 3-inch pots. *By permission of Mr J. B. Stevenson.*

stage the temperature to aim at is about 50°F., but a 45°F. minimum at night will do no harm. Some growers move them into cold frames immediately they are well established, but if this is done they need some protection against frost, and the night temperature should not be below 35°F.

About the middle of March the young plants should be ready to move into 5-inch pots, using J.I.P.$_2$. Cold frame protection is sufficient, but it will be wise to keep the lights on for a few days after potting. By about the end of April most varieties will have produced side shoots or 'breaks' and the tops should be 'stopped', that is, pinched out to put the strength into the side shoots and secure the required number. The most important potting operation, the move into finals, is usually done during May, and for this hard ramming is essential. At this point, the question of size of pot arises and a knowledge of the vigour and behaviour of varieties is important. For the less vigorous, 9-inch pots will be large enough, but for strong growers it is best to use 10-inch. The pot should only be filled half full when potting to allow for top dressing later with new compost. It is wise to water well an hour or so before potting so that watering should not be necessary for a week or so after. This gives the new roots time to enter the new soil. Staking should also be done before the young roots penetrate the new compost, to avoid damaging them.

Providing the weather is reasonably good the pots may go straight out to the summer quarters or standing ground. This is best prepared by levelling sharp weathered ashes; these ensure good drainage and do not encourage slugs and snails or worms to enter the pots through the drainage holes.

The site must be open and sunny, never under the shade of trees. The side of a path will serve admirably for small numbers. In either case, before the plants are stood out, posts and wires should be arranged to which the stakes may be tied to prevent damage by wind. The usual arrangement is one set of posts to two rows of plants and a 3-foot path between rows. Boards are nailed to the posts to form T-pieces providing a wire about 4 feet in height for each line of pots.

The best method of staking, though it does involve a good deal of labour and time, is to use three or more canes per plant, two

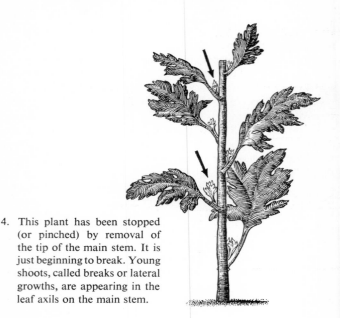

4. This plant has been stopped (or pinched) by removal of the tip of the main stem. It is just beginning to break. Young shoots, called breaks or lateral growths, are appearing in the leaf axils on the main stem.

of which are tied in to the wires, the third being loosely looped in. The young shoots are tied in to the canes as growth develops. In this way each bloom is held firmly and when developed cannot damage or bruise its neighbour by swaying about in the wind.

A great deal of time can be saved by selecting canes of approximately the height of the variety at maturity.

Stopping and Timing

If the plants are wanted for November most growers will root the cuttings early, even in December, and whether to take them on first or second crowns depends largely on the variety. This knowledge must be acquired either from the Chrysanthemum Growers' list or from the literature of the National Chrysanthemum Society. The preparation of plants for show work is outside the scope of this work, but there are excellent books dealing with the subjects.

5. Plant almost ready for disbudding. The centre bud developing at the end of each of the six breaks is the First Crown bud. The arrows indicate shoots that might be left in reserve until the First Crown bud is seen to be developing satisfactorily.

Stopping and its alternatives, 'pinching' and 'timing', merely mean taking out the tip of the shoot. If the first shoot is pinched out the result is called a natural break, the bud taken out being called the break bud. Three or more lateral shoots develop, being what are known as first crown buds. If these buds are pinched out to delay flowering the new buds produced are second crown buds.

The first stopping is usually done when the plants are established in 5-inch pots. The dates will vary quite a bit according to the district. The latter part of April would suit most southern and midland gardens; a little later in the north. For the majority of late-flowering varieties a second stopping is done about the middle or end of June. The plant should have three or four main branches and this second stopping will cause the plant to produce a larger number; eight, ten, or even more. How many the grower decides to leave to flower depends on his purpose and on the variety. If he wants blooms for show he will limit the number; if only for decorative purposes, he can allow more shoots to develop.

193

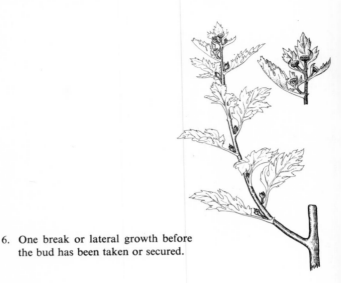

6. One break or lateral growth before the bud has been taken or secured.

Taking the Bud

This term or the equivalent, securing the bud, simply means disbudding or taking away all the smaller buds and shoots, leaving the selected bud to develop. If this is not done, as, for example, in some singles in which all buds are allowed to develop, the result is a spray. For November flowering the buds should be taken by about the middle of September. With later-flowering varieties it may be a week or two later.

Tying in

From the moment the selected buds are taken any small buds which develop and shoots which come from lower down the stem should be cut away. As the flower stems develop they must be looped in to the stake. This tying should be done regularly and carefully. The best method is to put the tying material twice round the cane to fix it in position and then loosely round the flower stem so that when the flower stem expands it will not be strangled.

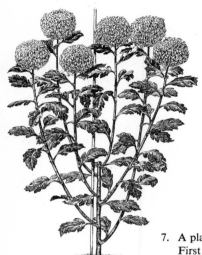

7. A plant carrying six blooms from
First Crown buds.

Watering and Feeding

From the time when the plants are stood out, watering must be attended to daily unless, of course, it is raining heavily. It is best done early in the day, and during hot weather it is wise to look over them again in the evening to make sure that none are flagging. The essential is that, when dry, the pots should be filled up and the ball thoroughly soaked.

Sufficient food is incorporated in a well-made compost to carry the plant to maturity, but regular feeding from about the end of June till buds are well developed will give the boost necessary to ensure first-class flowers. The safest plan is to rely on a balanced fertilizer prepared by a firm with a reputation, and if their recommendations as regards dosage are followed you cannot go far wrong. Don't ever imagine that because a little is good more is better. Never exceed the stated dose; even if there is no apparent damage it is still a waste of money.

The old, old rule in feeding is little and often, whatever method is used. The usual practice is to begin feeding when the plants

8. Plant stopped a second time by removal of the tip of each of the six first breaks. Young shoots called second breaks are appearing in the leaf axils.

   The inset shows the process of running on, and the rubbing out of the First Crown bud. Many growers now prefer to remove also the young shoot immediately below the First Crown bud and to allow the next lower shoot to run on to form a Second Crown bud.

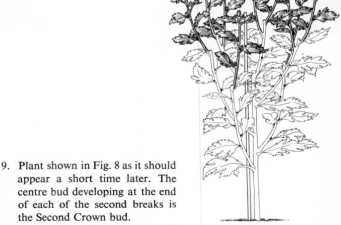

9. Plant shown in Fig. 8 as it should appear a short time later. The centre bud developing at the end of each of the second breaks is the Second Crown bud.

196

have been in their final pots about five or six weeks and the roots are well into the new compost. Start at once a week and gradually make it more frequent, though at reduced strength so that the stated amount is spread over the week. It is generally agreed that liquid feeding is safer than 'dry' feeds; that is, putting the fertilizer on the pots dry and relying on watering to wash it in.

When feeding roots show on the surface of the compost it is time to add top dressings of the prepared final compost. Provided sufficient space has been left in the pots for this, several such dressings may be given. Once the buds are well advanced the plants will make little growth and it is wise to reduce feeding. Overfeeding at this time can produce large but soft flowers.

Housing

If the greenhouse can be emptied before housing it should first be thoroughly cleaned and, if possible, the woodwork scrubbed down with a disinfectant. It is easier also at this time to deal with cracked panes or other minor repairs. Where J.I. potting composts are used it should not be necessary, but where acidity is suspected in the compost it is an old custom to water with dilute lime-water before housing.

The dates for carrying out this operation vary a good deal with locality. Where frosts are prevalent the end of September may be late enough, but in many localities they can be left till mid-October, though if colour is showing in the flower bud they are safer under cover.

Before housing it is a wise precaution to spray with a fungicide to check the development of mildew. Temperatures must be kept cool and relatively dry – a minimum of 45° F. is sufficient.

Chrysanthemum Varieties

The naming of new varieties is under the control of the National Chrysanthemum Society who compile and publish the national register of names. They are also responsible for the present system of classification and code of rules for judging. No new variety can be added to this register until vetted by the selection committee, and an unregistered variety will not be eligible for showing if the flower show is being judged under N.C.S. rules. Apart

109. Specimen plant of chrysanthemum 'Annie Curry' with 400 flowers.

from those grown out of doors for early flowering there are no less than seventeen different classes.

For show work it is essential to know something about the classification. The large mop heads formerly known as Japanese are known as Exhibition varieties. Incurves have all petals up-turned, decoratives are slightly smaller and may be either reflexed or incurved. Anemone-flowered have a ring of single ray florets with a closely packed mass of small florets in the centre often of a different colour.

Some of the loveliest of all are amongst the singles, they are defined as having not more than five rows of florets.

Varieties are so numerous and come and go with such rapidity today that a list of varieties may be no sooner in print than it is superseded.

A brief selection of popular varieties would include:

110. Large exhibition chrysanthemum 'Keith Luxford'.

Large Exhibition

White: 'Duke of Kent', 'Henry E. Trueman', 'Jessie Hab-good'.

Yellow: 'Golden Trueman', 'Yellow Trueman'.

Pink: 'Edith Woolman', Keith 'Luxford' (Plate 110).

Light Bronze: 'Chas. Shoesmith'.

Bronze: 'Majestic'.

Red: 'Red Majestic', 'James Bryant', 'Cossack'.

Reflexed decoratives

'Ulster', deep crimson; 'Shirley', garnet red; 'Shell Beauty', pale pink; 'Ada Stevens', golden.

Incurving decoratives

'Balcombe Perfection', orange and bronze; 'Pink Superb', 'Cream Lady', 'Golden Globe'.

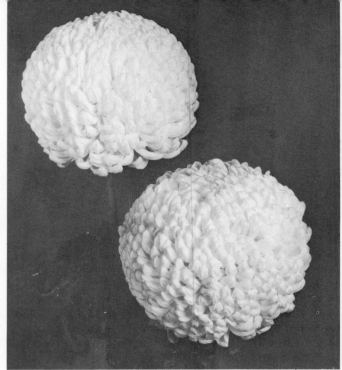

111. Incurved chrysanthemum 'Ron Shoesmith'.

Exhibition incurve

'Annie Curry', white (Plate 109), and Sports in yellow, buff, gold, pink, and lilac; 'Ondine', glistening white; 'Connie Mayhew', cream; 'Vera Woolman', yellow; 'Ron Shoesmith' (Plate 111), white; 'Shirley Primrose'.

Singles

'Peter Robinson', clear yellow; 'Rob Roy', crimson; 'Albert Cooper', yellow; 'J. H. Woodward', apricot; 'Broadacre', white.

Anemone-flowered singles

'Caleb Cox', amber and gold; 'Elspeth', mauve; 'Golden Nymph', 'Mabel Watson', white.

112. Reflexed decorative.

113. 'Charm' group of chrysanthemums.

Other groups of singles are the 'Charm' (Plate 113) and the 'Cascade' (Plate 114). The 'Charm' group have been largely raised from seed annually, and offer a fair range of colour. It is, however, only a matter of time before good forms are selected which will reproduce from cuttings. They form low, rounded bushes which when in flower become brilliant mounds of colour.

'Cascades' were at one time favoured, but they do require a good deal of training and are less popular today. They may be grown in the orthodox way on canes or inverted, that is, trained

114. 'Cascade' chrysanthemums trained downwards.

along canes with a downward inclination so that all flowers face outwards in one direction.

The 'Korean Race' also, though almost hardy, may be brought under glass to flower.

Pests and diseases are dealt with elsewhere, but there are unfortunately a few to which the chrysanthemum is especially prone.

Chrysanthemum gall midge can be very troublesome. Thorn-shaped galls are caused by the whitish larvae of the midge feeding inside the plant tissue. Usually the leaves only are affected, but sometimes stems, and also the flower, is in consequence distorted. In this case it is best to burn the plant, but in minor attacks regular spraying with D.D.T. should keep it under control.

Eelworm. Two species attack chrysanthemums. The one known as root knot eelworm causes the roots to swell and the plants to wilt in consequence. In commercial practice it can be controlled by Parathion, but to use this requires protective clothing and other precautions. For the amateur this is not worth while, and his best plan is to burn infected stock and make a fresh start with cuttings obtained from a reliable source. The other species is not quite so serious; this is the chrysanthemum eelworm which lives in the leaves. In affected plants the leaves at the bottom turn yellow, brown, and then black, and fall against the stem, gradually working up the plant. This can be controlled by treating the stools in winter in a hot-water bath. The stools should be washed to remove soil and then dipped in a bath of hot water. The older method was to keep them immersed at a temperature of 110°F. for thirty minutes, but it is now recommended that five minutes at 115°F. is better as it reduces the risk of damage in some varieties. After dipping, the stools are washed in clean cold water and boxed or planted in sterilized soil.

14 · Carnations

Perpetual Flowering

Like the chrysanthemum the modern carnation is of garden origin but a much more recent development. Though the wild species *Dianthus caryophyllus* is a native of Europe and was described so long ago as 300 B.C., the name carnation was not given until 1578. To what extent other species are involved in its development is not known, but it is almost certainly of hybrid origin.

The parent species were undoubtedly hardy or near-hardy plants and it is certain that the hardier carnations are grown, the better the results. They can be grown without heat, but then their greatest asset is lost. This is of course their value in flowering during the winter months under glass. The group most generally grown under glass in this country, the perpetual flowering race, were originally raised in France. They were first brought to this country about 1856. They were also taken to America and there rapidly became a popular flower, many of their best varieties coming back to Europe as American carnations.

Though carnations can be grown together with some other greenhouse plants they do require more sunshine and light than most, and it is usually better to grow them in a house by themselves.

How to start is sometimes a matter of economics, but though the cheapest way is to buy rooted cuttings it is often better in the long run to buy established plants in 6-inch pots. These provide flower almost at once and later plenty of propagation material. The beginner can also buy plants in 3-inch pots. If you are choosing varieties from a grower's list or from an exhibit at a show be careful not to buy too tall-growing varieties. There are a number with more stocky habit which are more suitable for a small house than are many of the varieties grown by the nurseryman for cut flowers.

The British National Carnation Society publishes a year book giving details of up-to-date varieties.

Cultivation

The first essential for successful cultivation of carnations is a light, airy, and well-ventilated greenhouse. For pot-grown plants hard benches covered with gravel or ashes are preferable to prevent too rapid drying out. Too dry conditions also favour the development of red spider, one of the worst enemies of carnations. During sunny summer weather the atmosphere should be kept moist by damping and syringing, and with small houses light shading is necessary for flowering plants, especially during a heat-wave. A light tiffany screen inside the house is usually sufficient. Some growers use whitening on the glass, but it should not remain on in dull weather and a temporary shading which can be removed in the evening is best.

During the winter the atmosphere must be kept drier. In dull weather a low temperature with plenty of air circulating is better for the plants than a high temperature. During damp, muggy weather a little more artificial heat is necessary to keep the air moving and the atmosphere moderately dry. A little ventilation on the leeward side is always desirable during the day. A night minimum of 45°F. is sufficient and a fall to 40°F., though not desirable, will do no great harm. The temperature during the day need never be higher than 50°F.

While the pots are better on the dry side in winter, care must be taken that they do not become so dry that feeding roots die. Watering should be done in the morning so that surplus moisture may be dried up during the warmest part of the day.

For the amateur with a small house there is still a difference of opinion as to whether it is better to grow in pots or to plant in prepared borders as is done by the large growers.

The advantage of pot cultivation is that they are portable. They can, if desired, be plunged out of doors or preferably in frames. Where planting out is to be practised it is best to do it when the plant is small, in fact it may be done straight from the propagating case into a 5- or 6-inch-deep prepared bed. Usually they are first established in 3-inch pots and planted later. It is, however, more of a check to allow them to become pot-bound, that is, too full of roots, before moving on.

During the summer pot-grown plants are quite happy in cold

frames, the advantage is that the lights can be pulled off in fine sunny weather and only used to protect them from heavy rains. They are often stood out on an ash bed but a wet summer will make growth too soft.

Potting

If they are to be grown in pots the usual procedure is potting on into 3-inch, then 5-inch and finally about June into 6- or 7-inch pots – or in the case of two-year-old plants, into 8- or 9-inch pots.

The essentials are clean washed pots and firm potting. Under no circumstances should a plant be potted when it is too dry or into too dry composts. Too wet is as bad or worse! Nor should the neck of the plant be potted lower than in the cutting pot. If it is buried it will probably fall a victim to stem rot in winter. Lastly, see that the drainage at the bottom of the pot is good. If you skip a size and give them a larger move, then you must be extremely careful with the water-pot. In any case watering should not be done for forty-eight hours after potting on.

Potting Compost

There is no doubt that good-quality carnations can be grown in John Innes composts, but most growers dislike using peat. They prefer a mixture of loam with sand and mortar rubble or limestone chips. If the loam is of good quality the proportion is 4 loam to 1 of the other materials. A proprietary carnation fertilizer is added as recommended by the makers. For rooted cuttings a higher proportion of sand should be used for the first potting; if the loam is heavy it may be as much as half and half. Lime in some form is essential, as the parent species are lime lovers and they will not tolerate acid soil conditions. Where it can be obtained, lime rubble, broken up and screened, is probably the best way of incorporating lime, as it improves·drainage at the same time.

Feeding

Given a good compost and a frequent potting on, carnations should not require much artificial feeding. The only period when this may be justified is when the flowering size pot is becoming filled with roots in late summer. It is unwise to continue into autumn, as excessive growth is not then required. General plant fertilizers are not desirable because they generally contain too much nitrogen and so stimulate too much foliage and tend to make growth soft. The safest course (for the private grower) is to use a proprietary fertilizer made for carnations and used strictly as recommended by the makers.

Propagation

This has been made very easy today for the amateur. Specially made propagating cases are available with soil-heating cables for providing bottom heat. Failing one of these de luxe models a simple frame can be fixed up or even one of the glass 'cloches' adapted for the purpose. The barn-type cloche is suitable if closed at the ends. Air can be readily admitted as the cuttings become rooted. Where a large number of cuttings are being inserted it is more economical to prepare a cutting bed or to insert them in 4-inch-deep clay pans. For smaller quantities 5-inch pots are usually best, though these should be plunged to the rims in ashes or sand. The material most generally used is sharp sand, which must be clean and well firmed when inserting the cuttings.

Cutting propagation is most generally used for perpetual flowering carnations. The most important point is that the parent stock should be clean and healthy and it is almost equally important that only selected short-jointed cuttings should be used. These are generally pulled off with a heel (Plate 115), which is trimmed with a knife and the two lowest pairs of leaves cut off (Plate 116). About $\frac{3}{4}$ inch is sufficient depth to insert and about $\frac{1}{2}$ inch apart (Plate 117). They must be watered immediately to firm and consolidate the sand. The lights should be left open for a while for the surplus water to dry off. They should then be closed, lightly shaded, and given a daily look over and airing until they show signs of rooting, when a little air can be given. The amount is gradually increased until the lights can be left off. They should be potted off at the earliest possible moment after rooting, as there is no nutriment whatever in the sand. For a few

115. Choosing a cutting. Note the place on the plant from which it has been taken.

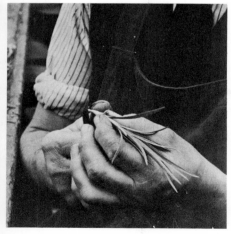

116. Trimming the cutting.

117. Inserting cuttings.

days shading may be necessary, but once they are growing, full light and plenty of air must be given.

Cuttings rooted cool, say 45°F., will always make better and more short-jointed plants than those rooted in higher temperatures, but there is no doubt that a little bottom heat is beneficial and hastens rooting (Plate 118). Cuttings are usually taken from

118. Potting off rooted cuttings.

December onwards for plants to flower the following autumn and winter. Under town conditions where winter light is poor it is wiser to root cuttings in October.

Successional batches may be taken in January and February. Some growers contend that constant propagation by cuttings weakens the stock and that the old-fashioned method of layering is the best, with perpetuals as with borders. They claim that the young plants from layers get away more quickly and build up larger plants. The plant may be knocked out of its pot and planted in a cold frame, on its side, so that all shoots may be layered. Alternatively, the lower shoots may be layered directly into the new compost round the rim of a newly potted plant. For this layering a cold frame is best. All leaves except the six terminal ones are stripped off and a tongue cut from a joint (or node) two joints below the lowest leaves left on the layer.

By the way, the cut may be done either upwards or by inserting the knife blade through the stem and cutting downwards. In either case trim the tongue off level just below the joint, press it into the soil ½ inch or so deep, and make it secure and firm with a wire pin. When all are inserted, mound over them with fine soil, and water in with a rose to firm the soil. The time required for rooting varies from a month to six weeks.

Stopping

For general cultivation they are generally 'stopped'; that is, the top is broken clean out when the plant begins to elongate about early March, leaving 4 to 6 inches of stem (Plate 119). This causes a number of shoots to break and a bushy type of plant results. These young growths would of course produce flowers, but in order to spread the flowering period they are again stopped, but gradually, a few at a time. To stop the growths all at once would be a considerable check, and it would also cause a second crop of shoots which would again tend to flower all together, so a gradual process of stopping is practised until about the end of June or early July. Stopping is best done in the morning while stems are turgid and brittle. They should not be pinched out, as that bruises the stem, but turned over and snapped off.

119. Stopping. This plant should have been stopped earlier.

Disbudding

When the crown bud is developing a number of lateral buds are also produced and the practice of disbudding must be regularly carried out. If these buds were left it would not only spoil the main flower but the resulting side growths would be short-stemmed and poor. All laterals are therefore removed when large enough to pick off easily, and the material and energy directed into one good flower. This should be done gradually by going over the plants once or twice a week and rubbing the buds out. When doing so, care is needed not to damage the guard leaves. The buds should be taken out from the leaf axis on a tangent to the main stem.

Staking and Tying

One feature of carnation growing which has changed appreciably in recent years is tying in. In the old private carnation houses each shoot was carefully looped in to a stake, and tying went on all summer. Today a good strong stake and a few wire rings take care of the problem, though the unruly shoots have to be poked and persuaded to keep within the fold. Where the plants are grown in beds the solution is even simpler; wires are fixed at convenient heights and strings run through to form a network sufficient to support the flowers. New strings are of course added as the plants increase in height. This system makes cutting a simple job; whereas with tied-in flowers each flower has to be cut free.

Second-year Plants

If flower stems are cut long, as they usually are, little pruning is necessary in carrying plants on for the second year. Provided the plants are clean and healthy this is quite worth while. Re-potting should be done not later than June to give them time to re-establish before autumn.

They can be moved on into 8- or 9-inch pots or, if already in this size, the ball may be reduced and repotted into the same size pots.

VARIETIES. As with all specialized flowers there are an enormous number of varieties from which to choose, and each year new ones are added. Most people will prefer the pure self colours, but there are many other classes and they have a vocabulary of their own. Fancies, Flakes, and Bizarres are all striped or flaked on to a self colour, while Picotees are self colours with a rim of another colour. For show purposes these have to be studied carefully.

Carnations may be raised from seed, but the chance of raising new varieties of value is remote because so many thousands have been raised to provide the chosen few which come before the selection committee annually. Nevertheless, first-class varieties have been raised by private growers, and in any case hybridizing.

120. Carnation 'William Sim'.

121. Carnation 'Miller's Yellow'.

sowing, and raising, no matter what the flower may be, is one of the most fascinating phases of gardening. Sowing must be done in January or February if results are to be seen the same year. Annual carnations are referred to under 'Plants from Seed' (p. 136).

MALMAISON CARNATIONS. The old type of Malmaison produced only one crop of flowers per year and was always propagated by layering, after flowering. The newer race called Perpetual Malmaison have a longer flowering season. They require similar treatment to the perpetual flowering and may be propagated either by cuttings or layers. They require more root room, at least a 6-inch pot for a one-year-old and a 10-inch for a two-year-old.

Carnation Pests and Diseases

The two most troublesome pests are thrips and red spider. Both flourish under hot and dry conditions and, fortunately for us, both dislike forcible syringing. The remedy therefore is to use the syringe as freely as possible during the summer whenever the weather conditions justify it.

An old but effective deterrent is to sprinkle flake naphthalene along damp paths. This is best done in the evening, while the house is at a reasonably high temperature, say about 70°F., and the house closed until morning.

If in spite of these measures spider does get a hold, fumigation with Azobenzine smokes is the easiest and best way of dealing with it. B.H.C. smokes will control thrips and also any aphis which may be about.

Too much humidity and overwatering sometimes causes attacks of Carnation Rust, brown powdery marks on the leaves. With pot-grown plants any infected plants should be isolated and the affected leaves should be picked off and burned to destroy spores. The plants should be dusted with a powder fungicide or, in summer, sprayed with one of the new proprietary fungicides at the strengths advised by the makers.

15 · Pests and Diseases

In no phase of horticulture has so much progress been made as in the control of pests. The once highly unpleasant and often dangerous business of fumigation has now become simplicity itself. Some insecticides used are highly poisonous and one in particular, Parathion, is at present too risky to recommend. Others of the same group, the organo-phosphorus compounds, need care in use, and some people are more sensitive to their effects than others. In every case it is essential to study and follow implicitly the maker's directions.

Fumigation

This is the quickest and most effective remedy for dealing with most insect pests under glass. Fumigation of the house should be regular. The first essential is to find the cubic capacity of the house and keep a note of it. First measure the height to the ridge and to the gutter. Add these together and divide by two to get the average height, multiply this by the length of the house and then by the width. Having the cubic capacity of the house, any sundriesman can supply 'smokes' of a suitable size.

Next look over the house for faults in the ventilators, doors, etc., and if these are not fitting tightly pack them with paper or rags. Replace any cracked or broken glass or make a temporary repair by laying or tacking another sheet over it. It is best to fumigate on a windless evening and with a reasonably high inside temperature, say 60° F. to 70° F. Leave the house locked and tightly closed until the following morning, when as much ventilation should be given as the weather allows.

Smokes

These are made in the form of pellets for small houses and canisters of assorted sizes for larger. They rather suggest Guy Fawkes' day and are in fact lighted in the same way as the familiar 'squib'. It is only necessary to take off the paper cap and light the wick with a match or lighter. They are now available in a whole range of chemical compounds designed to deal effectively with different pests, and have greatly simplified pest control.

For the commoner greenhouse pests, aphis, thrips, leaf hoppers, and leaf miners, one of the B.H.C. (benzine hexachloride) group is recommended, particularly the form called Lindane or Lindane and D.D.T. combined. This cannot be used safely with any of the marrow, melon, or cucumber family, or with tomatoes or roses. White fly is very resistant to most fumigants, but two or three applications of these combined 'smokes' at fourteen days' interval should get rid of them. Though not strictly an insect, red spider is dealt with in the same way by using an Azobenzine smoke. Plants which may be damaged by this are sweet peas, schizanthus, and zinnias, pilea, and asparagus, but it is safe with the majority of greenhouse plants.

Insecticides

Liquid insecticides are also available in a bewildering range. Most of them are lethal to a number of insect pests. In using an insecticide these are the important points: first, follow exactly the directions of the makers as regards dilution, and mix thoroughly; secondly, deal with an infestation immediately it is noticed; thirdly, cover every part of the plant. Two types of insecticide are required. For the sucking group of insects, such as aphis, a contact wash is applied with some force to envelop the bodies of the insects. For the other group which actually eat the foliage, for example, caterpillars, a stomach poison applied as a fine spray is necessary so that every part of the plant is covered, and, in feeding, the insect is bound to eat the poison. For this purpose nicotine has always been the best control, but is now being superseded by what are called organo-phosphorus compounds. They are first-class contact and stomach poisons, but require care in handling, as they are still poisonous both to humans and domestic animals.

Two of these are H.E.T.P. (hexa-ethyl-tetra-phosphate) and T.E.P.P. (tetra-ethyl-pyro-phosphate). They may be used at low temperatures (which nicotine cannot), but should be used immediately as they quickly break down after dilution. Malathion,

122. An Aerovap in a mixed plant house.

another compound of this group, promises to be particularly effective in controlling sucking insects.

White oil emulsions are useful on tough and leathery-leaved foliage, but can damage plants with a waxy surface such as carnations. The best known of these is Volck; its oily nature produces a wonderful shine on evergreen foliage.

Two other developments in the control of insect pests are the Aeroside and Aerovap. In the first a projector charged with insecticide and liquid gas is used. When released the gas comes out with sufficient force to disperse small droplets of insecticide over the whole of the greenhouse. Aerovaps are thermostatically controlled containers heated by electricity to such a point that vapour containing insecticide is constantly present in the atmosphere of the house (Plate 122). In houses freely ventilated they can be switched on while the house is closed or partly closed at night. The great advantage of these over the older methods is that every particle of foliage is covered with a toxic material and no insect can escape the deadly vapour. Chemical compounds used can, of course, be varied to deal with different pests. Both systems can also be used to vaporize fungicides.

One new line of research is in what are termed systemic insecticides in which the chemicals are actually absorbed into the sap of the plant, making the plant itself toxic to insects. This at present can only be done effectively in high temperatures and is in the experimental stage, but it has possibilities. It has one great advantage over the orthodox insecticides: it only kills sucking insects and not predators which feed on them. While these insecticides are potentially valuable they have not been in use long enough for real assessment and they should certainly be used with caution.

'Dusting' with powder insecticides is another method of control. These dusts are lighter to handle than water-borne liquids but require an efficient machine to ensure an even distribution. This method of application is perhaps most useful in nipping in the bud small and local infestations. Much the same range of chemical combinations is available as for fumigation, and for most insects D.D.T. and B.H.C. are effective. The latter is now superseding the older Derris and Pyrethrum dusts.

I would have preferred not to give a list of pests and diseases. There appear to be so many that they might make the beginner wonder whether he can cope with them. He need not fear on that score, given good cultivation and hygiene and using modern methods of control. At the same time forewarned is forearmed, and if he is on the look-out for pests he will spot them and deal with them before they ever become serious.

ANTS do a good deal of mechanical damage by tunnelling and moving soil about. They can be troublesome particularly with cacti and succulents, where they find the dry atmospheric conditions to their liking. They are also responsible for the spread of mealy bug and aphides. Dusts of benzine hexachloride (B.H.C.) or D.D.T. are the most effective. They are sprinkled in the runs and at the entrance to the nests. B.H.C. smokes will kill ants caught above ground.

APHIDS, variously known as blight, green and black flies, and plant lice, are amongst the most prolific of all insect pests. They attack all kinds of plants both under glass and in the open, and the damage caused is mainly by sucking the plant sap. They also are known to transmit diseases from plant to plant, and their secretions encourage the growth of the unsightly sooty moulds, which in turn check the breathing pores of the plant.

It is, however, their extremely rapid rate of increase which makes constant vigilance so necessary. Aphids are protected by nature in a way which causes solutions in water to run off them and a 'spreader' or wetting agent has to be added to the insecticide to prevent this. The older insecticides, particularly nicotine, with a good spreader, and Derris preparations still give control, but are being superseded by B.H.C., H.E.T.P., and T.E.P.P. Routine fumigation with one of the newer B.H.C. smokes gives good control, but D.D.T. is not effective either as smokes or sprays.

CATERPILLARS. Several species of moth larvae may at times be found feeding on indoor plants, but a dusting of D.D.T. dust is usually sufficient to deal with these, or, alternatively, D.D.T. as a contact spray.

COCKROACHES. At least two species of these insects frequent the warm corners of the greenhouse and can cause damage by feeding on the roots and tender foliage of plants. Specially designed traps are made to deal with them, and a poison bait of Paris green and bran is an old but effective remedy. They are killed by smokes if caught by them, but they are usually either too well hidden or too mobile for these to be regarded as controls. D.D.T. or B.H.C. dusts scattered in their haunts are also partial controls.

LEAF HOPPERS. These can be destructive with greenhouse plants, particularly soft foliage plants like calceolaria and primula. They come into the 'sucking' group and are best controlled by fumigation with one of the B.H.C. group of smokes or forcible syringing with an insecticide either of the same kind or H.E.T.P. or T.E.P.P.

LEAF MINERS. These are the larvae of small flies which lay their eggs on the undersides of the leaves. The larvae bore their way inside the leaf tissue, causing the familiar mines particularly

123. Leaf Miner damage.

124. Mealy Bug, adults and nymphs.

in the leaves of chrysanthemums and cinerarias (Plate 123). Again the most effective control is by fumigation, using B.H.C., or routine spraying with a preparation of the same material from April onwards.

MEALY BUG. The most difficult of all insect pests to eradicate under glass is mealy bug (Plate 124). Some of the Lindane compounds are giving good results; so are H.E.T.P. and T.E.P.P. The new Malathion is also giving excellent results. It is above all the pest that the amateur should avoid if possible. Examine every new acquisition and make certain that this pest is not introduced. It is usually cheaper and better to destroy a plant found infested than to keep it and risk spreading. With hard-wooded plants and palms it is safe to use a white oil emulsion which soon cleans them up, but with soft-foliage plants this is risky and the old-fashioned nicotine spray is still as effective as any. It is of course extremely poisonous and needs care in handling. On plants with a smooth skin, such as most succulents, forcible syringing with water will clean them off quickly and effectively, though, except during summer, care must be taken not to saturate the roots. In winter, touching them with a fine brush dipped in methylated spirit, though more laborious, is safer.

It is probable that a systemic insecticide such as Pestox will prove one of the most effective means of control. The Aerovap and Aerosol methods can also give complete control.

MICE can be devastating if they get amongst newly sown seeds, and they can cause a good deal of damage amongst bulbs. Trapping is usually effective. With the field mouse soaked peas will be found the best bait.

MILLEPEDES (Plate 125). Several species may be found feeding on roots and foliage, and they are particularly troublesome on bulbs. The old-fashioned but effective method of trapping with cut potatoes or other vegetables should be used if D.D.T. does not give control.

MITES. Red spider mite (Plate 126) is rarely troublesome where a humid atmosphere is maintained, but under dry

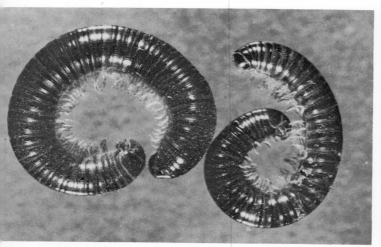

125. Millepedes.

126. Red Spider mite, adults, eggs, and young mites.

conditions it increases rapidly. The Azobenzine smoke canister makes it an easy pest to control, though there are certain plants which may be damaged by their use.

The mites are extremely small and the first sign of attack is usually the spotting of the foliage. They feed on the undersides of the leaves and build up an infestation incredibly quickly. Dry litter of any kind should be avoided, particularly old canes, boxes, and flower pots left lying about. Where smokes cannot be used the contact insecticides H.E.T.P. and T.E.P.P. should be used.

Begonia mite causes distortion in the foliage of begonias, cyclamen, fuchsias, and other plants. Dusting with fine sulphur dust immediately it is noticed still seems to be the best means of control on a small scale and sulphur vaporization on a larger.

Another species attacks ferns; for these, flaked naphthaline is effective, though it cannot be used with adiantums. It should be applied when the temperature is high, about 70° F., and sprinkled on damp floors. The house should be kept close and damp for twenty-four hours.

SCALE INSECTS (Plate 127). These differ from most insect pests in that for the greater part of their lives they are inactive. The body is protected by a scaly covering which makes them difficult to dislodge. The most vulnerable moment in their life history is when they are young and active. Regular fumigation or syringing with an insecticide will catch them in this stage. Ants also should be checked, as they 'farm' them for the honeydew which these insects deposit. Moulds also develop on this honeydew and make the plants unsightly and unhealthy. There are several species which attack greenhouse plants. Apart from frequent fumigation I know of no better control than the old-fashioned nicotine soap. On palms and plants with similar tough foliage a white oil emulsion combined with nicotine can be used, but this is not safe on many soft-foliage plants. In a bad infestation sponging the plants and dislodging the scale may have to be practised. Systemic insecticides afford a promising method of control, and Malathion has also given good results and will probably supersede nicotine.

127. Scale insects.

SLUGS AND SNAILS. These creatures can be most destructive, particularly amongst newly germinated seedlings, and are often difficult to locate. The metaldehyde compounds now on the market are extremely effective. The only thing the gardener has to do is put this material down at night where it will not get too wet and pick up and destroy the 'bag' in the morning. Metaldehyde is also prepared in liquid form, and this can be sprinkled over floors, frames, etc., with a fine-rosed can. Hygiene is also important, as weeds and rubbish lying about will harbour them.

THRIPS are small sucking insects which are all too frequently not noticed until damage is serious. There are several species and they will attack almost any greenhouse plant. They may be black, brown, or yellow, and are not more than one-tenth of an inch long. Breeding is rapid under warm conditions. Fumigation with either

D.D.T. or Lindane is effective, and on many plants a white oil emulsion may be used. This should, however, not be used on soft-foliage plants or on flowering plants of cyclamen, carnations, or arums, as it will spoil the flowers.

They dislike wet conditions, and repeated forcible syringing is the most economical means of control where it can be done.

WEEVILS. In this particular pest it is the larva, a white usually curved grub, which does most damage. It is often found attacking the roots of cyclamen and fleshy-rooted plants like primulas. The grubs are not easy to detect until the plant is on the verge of collapse. First-aid treatment is to shake out the plant and try and re-root it, and consign the whole of the ball and soil to the bonfire. Where they have previously been troublesome a few crystals of benzine hexachloride or dieldrin dust, $1\frac{1}{2}$ oz. per bushel, should be put into the soil when potting, or crystals of paradichlorobenzine placed round the collar of the plant. There are also preparations of B.H.C. which may be diluted and watered into the soil. The adult weevil also feeds on vegetation, but is rarely seen, as it hides during the day and feeds at night. It may be trapped in pieces of dry sacking or similar materials.

WHITE FLY have always been one of the most difficult of insect pests to keep in check in greenhouses. Fumigation with D.D.T. smokes or D.D.T./Lindane will control adults but not eggs. It has therefore to be repeated at intervals of fourteen days to catch those emerging from eggs, until the infestation is under control. The only reliable fumigant which could previously be used on most greenhouse plants, hydrocyanic acid gas, was always dangerous. What is known as biological control is widely employed, especially on tomato crops. A small chalcid wasp, *Encarsia formosa*, is introduced to the house and preys on the pupae of the white fly. If this is not readily available the County Horticultural Adviser will usually be able to put you in touch with a source of supply.

WIREWORMS. The sterilization of composts has more or less eliminated this pest under glass, but it can easily be introduced in loam which is not sterilized. The larvae feed on plant roots. If it should be found in pot-plants, crystals of paradichlorobenzine on the surface of the pots will kill them, or B.H.C. soil insecticide.

WOODLICE are more destructive than is generally realized, feeding on stems, leaves, and roots. They are controlled by B.H.C. or D.D.T. dusts dusted under the stages and out-of-the-way corners of the house. They are killed by D.D.T. or Lindane smokes if exposed, but they are usually too securely hidden to be caught. Cleanliness under the stages is most important, as litter or plant debris provides them with breeding grounds.

FUNGAL DISEASES are either saprophytes living on dead tissue or parasites obtaining their food direct from a living host plant. They are reproduced by minute spores which are carried from place to place by currents of air. Like the plants on which they live, many of them flourish on warm, damp conditions. Control is either by spraying or dusting with fungicides chiefly composed of copper salts or sulphur with other chemicals and in a wide range of proprietary makes. For most greenhouse plants they are not generally a serious matter, though individual plants such as carnation, chrysanthemum, and tomatoes may be badly affected.

DAMPING OFF. PYTHIUM SPP. This is most troublesome with seedlings. The best control is thin sowing, but as a preventive Cheshunt Compound should be used in watering seed pots and boxes and again when transplanting. This is a copper fungicide made by mixing 2 parts copper sulphate with 11 parts powdered ammonium carbonate. It is readily available from the sundriesman, but should be stored in glass jars or bottles. To use, dissolve 1 oz. in warm water and dilute to 2 gallons, using while fresh. The use of sterilized soil such as J.I. composts is also a preventive.

MILDEWS. In these the plants become covered with a white fungal growth. Good ventilation is the best preventive. Sprays of either sulphur fungicides or colloidal copper or dusts of sulphur will give control but may have to be repeated. A new preparation has been recently introduced which promises even better control. This is at present known as Karathane and may be used either as a spray or in the form of smoke cones.

MOULD. *Botrytis cinerea* often attacks soft-foliage plants such as pelargoniums and cyclamen in frames. The immediate remedy is better ventilation and drier conditions and the immediate removal of all affected foliage. Sulphur fungicides are again the best control.

RUSTS are well known, particularly on carnations and chrysanthemums, as orange patches on the foliage and stems. Proprietary sprays and dusts are made for use against these, those of colloidal copper being usually most effective.

Index

232

233

234

238